The Rockford Institute

The Rockford Institute seeks to be a leading force in establishing the principles needed to sustain a free society. Through research, conferences, and publications, the Institute influences the moral and intellectual forces that shape social and cultural trends and public issues. The Institute has programs in the general areas of religion and society, the family, and literature. It is a non-profit, tax-exempt educational organization.

Publications

Chronicles: A Magazine of American Culture — A monthly magazine that considers the influence of ideas, arts, and letters upon the character and viability of American society.

The Family in America — In-depth analysis each month of a topic of long-range importance to the family and democratic capitalism; includes news and information.

The Religion & Society Report — A monthly newsletter surveying events, trends, and publications across the religious spectrum that influence American culture and public issues.

Main Street Memorandum — A quarterly newsletter of Institute achievements for contributors and friends, contains important op-ed placements.

Communication

Institute research is especially adapted for newspaper editorial pages. Articles have appeared recently in The Wall Street Journal, USA Today, The Los Angeles Times, The Washington Post, the Chicago Tribune, the Chicago Sun-Times, the Houston Chronicle, and numerous other newspapers throughout the country. Staff articles have appeared in The Public Interest, National Review, Policy Review, Regulation, The American Spectator, Reason, and other journals of scholarship and opinion. Talk-show appearances by Institute staff include CBS Nightly News, NBC News, ABC's Nightline, William Buckley's Firing Line, CNN, CBN's 700 Club, National Public Radio, and numerous local television and radio programs.

Administration

Allan C. Carlson, president of the Institute; Michael Y. Warder, executive vice president; Bryce J. Christensen, director of the Institute Center on the Family in America, editor of The Family in America; Thomas J. Fleming, editor of Chronicles; John A. Howard, counselor to the Institute and director of the Ingersoll program; and Harold O.J. Brown, director of The Center on Religion & Society, editor of The Religion & Society Report.

Board of Directors

William Andrews (Chairman), William Nelson (Vice Chairman), Allan Carlson, Clayton Gaylord, Mary Kohler, Robert Krieble, Norman P. McClelland, Dallin Oaks, George O'Neill, Jr., Henry Regnery, Robert Sandblom, Clyde Sluhan, James Bond Stockdale, Kathleen M. Sullivan, Katherine M. Swim, and Frederick G. Wacker, Jr.

For more information:

Michael Warder, executive vice president; The Rockford Institute, 934 North Main Street, Rockford, Illinois 61103; (815) 964-5811.

The Family Research Council

Family Research Council, a division of Focus on the Family, is an independent non-profit, non-partisan organization in Washington, D.C., which provides an active and unifying voice for the pro-family movement. FRC strives to ensure that family interests are considered and respected in the formation of public policy.

Government Relations.

Every day, officials in Washington conduct hearings, pass legislation and make decisions that directly impact the family. FRC promotes the pro-family agenda in both the legislative and executive branches of the federal government.

Research/Policy Development.

FRC provides policy-makers with credible research data to support traditional family values. When government agencies or the media call for expert testimony from a pro-family perspective, FRC refers credible professionals from an extensive research resource network.

Media.

Increasingly, the media present a distorted view of family issues, often showing outright bias against traditional values. We have created an alternate voice—a spokesman for the family in the media. Our press releases and reactions frequently appear in the national media, including The Washington Post, The New York Times, the McNeil/Lehrer Newshour and Ted Koppel's Nightline.

Coalition Building.

FRC works to educate citizens about issues that affect the family, enabling them to influence their community and country on behalf on Judeo-Christian principles. FRC serves as an adviser to state and local groups as well, supplying them with information and political expertise.

Profile of the President.

FRC President Gary Bauer served former President Reagan as Director of the White House Office of Policy Development. Prior to that, Mr. Bauer served as Under Secretary of the U.S. Department of Education under Bill Bennett.

Publications.

Washington Watch: A monthly newsletter which focuses on current family issues in the Nation's Capital; Family Policy: A bi-monthly publication containing in-depth analysis of major policy issues and trends.

For more information:

Family Research Council, 700 Thirteenth Street, N.W., Suite 500, Washington, D.C. 20005 (202) 393-2100

When Families Fail . . . The Social Costs

Edited by Bryce J. Christensen

Based on a Conference Co-sponsored by

The Family Research Council, Washington, D.C.
and
The Rockford Institute, Rockford, Illinois

UNIVERSITY
PRESS OF
AMERICA

Lanham • New York • London

THE FAMILY
IN AMERICA

RESEARCH SERIES

The Rockford Institute

36.00

5-17-91

"Family Dissolution and the Health Care Crisis"
copyright © 1990 by Armand M. Nicholi

Library of Congress Cataloging-in-Publication Data

When families fail... the social costs / edited by Bryce J.
Christensen ; based on a conference co-sponsored by the Family
Research Council, Washington, D.C. and the Rockford Institute,
Rockford, Illinois.
        p.   cm.
     Includes index.
     1. Family—United States—Congresses.
  2. Family—Economic aspects—United States—Congresses.
  3. Family—Health and hygiene—United States—Congresses.
     4. Family policy—United States—Congresses.
          HQ536.W514   1990
     306.85'0973—dc20   90-27569 CIP

ISBN 0-8191-8140-4 (alk. paper)
ISBN 0-8191-8141-2 (pbk.: alk. paper)

Contents

For Katherine Swim,
a gracious friend of the American family.

Introduction

Family life has changed remarkably in the United States during the past thirty years. Since 1960, the divorce rate (per 1,000 married women, ages 15 and over) has more than doubled, while the marriage rate (per 1,000 unmarried women, ages 15 to 44) has fallen by almost 50 percent. While only 5 percent of all births in 1960 were illegitimate, about 25% of all births are now out of wedlock. Single-adult households accounted for only 13 percent of all households in 1960, but made up 24 percent of all American households in 1985.[1] While some Americans view these trends with deep concern, others gladly welcome the growing diversity in domestic lifestyles. What some regard as a dangerous threat to society, others interpret as a long overdue liberation of personal preferences. Among the institutions expressing concern about the implications of new patterns of family life, The Rockford Institute, Rockford, Illinois, and The Family Research Council, Washington, D.C., convened a conference in October 1989 at the Clock Tower Inn in Rockford, Illinois, to assess "The Social Costs of Family Dissolution."

The seventeen men and women in attendance at the conference came from various professional backgrounds—including sociology, psychology, economics, history, law, and journalism. But all present shared a deep interest in the changing character of American family life, although participants did not all agree about the meaning or consequences of current trends. No one present felt that divorce and illegitimacy were beneficial or desirable, but no consensus emerged about the causes of these breakdowns of family life nor about what measures—if any—government ought to adopt to reduce their incidence.

Author of the first paper presented at the conference, Professor Armand M. Nicholi, Jr. of Harvard Medical School reported that family dissolution causes tremendous emotional trauma among children and young people, leaving them vulnerable to despondency and mental illness. In his own clinical experience Nicholi had seen many children of divorced parents fail in school, fail in marriages, and succumb to the temptation to use drugs. Marveling at the way many fathers—and now increasingly mothers—neglect their children and homes, Nicholi feared that too many Americans are forgetting the two great commandments in Scripture (cf. Matt. 22: 37-39; Deut. 6:15; Lev. 19:18): the relationships that define the meaning of our brief time on earth.

But public policy—not religious reflection—defined the issues most debated. Serving as chairman for the conference, Douglas Besharov guided discussion of a number of policy questions. Should divorce be made more difficult or even outlawed? Does the welfare system need overhaul—or even abolishment? How has tax policy affected the family? When government intervenes to help employed women, how does that affect the wages and social status of men— especially black men?

In the second paper of the conference, Professor Sara McLanahan of the University of Wisconsin—Madison outlined some of the reasons that policymakers cannot ignore these family issues. Compared to children from intact families, children from single-parent households are more likely to drop out of high school, more likely to commit delinquent acts, more likely to have children out of wedlock, more likely to rely on welfare, more likely to divorce if they do marry. Not surprisingly, children from single-parent households do not do as well in school or in their careers as children from intact families.

Examining another problem—crime—often traced to family disintegration, Professor Travis Hirschi of the University of Arizona painted a complex and provocative picture. A statistical correlation does exist between family dissolution and delinquency, but it is not particularly strong, Hirschi noted, arguing that individual self-control is more important than family structure in preventing crime. Though largely in agreement, criminologist Robert Sampson of the University of Illinois wondered if Hirschi had not understated the importance of family in his analysis of crime, since family dissolution affects not only the immediate household, but also the neighborhood and community. Hirschi stirred a much stronger reaction when he reported a strong statistical correlation between family size and teen delinquency. A number of participants supposed that children of large families would not be particularly prone to delinquency if their parents were religiously motivated.

My own paper in this volume analyzes the ways in which the erosion of family life causes illnesses and drives up health-care costs. Some participants complained that I confused correlation and causation when looking at the relationship between divorce and disease, but all agreed that family dissolution increased the likelihood that taxpayers will bear the burden of health care.

McLanahan lays out the two fundamental options in public policy for dealing with the social costs of family dissolution: 1) the state could outlaw divorce while also perhaps coercing unwed fathers to marry; 2) the state could offer more meliorative services to women and children in single-parent households. McLanahan judged the first option an unjustified restriction of individual freedom. On the other hand, she admitted that increased government benefits for single-parent households would probably encourage more women to divorce or not to marry. McLanahan herself favored tightening of divorce laws along with new measures to provide subsidized day care and to raise pay for employed women.

More radical policy agendas also received attention during the conference. Borrowing a thought experiment from Charles Murray, historian Allan Carlson of The Rockford Institute wondered what would happen if the welfare state were simply dismantled. Wouldn't everyone—including the poor—then choose to marry and live in families because of the natural economic strengths of families? Although McLanahan dismissed this line of thought as undesirable and politically irrelevant, not everyone agreed. Economist Richard Vedder of Ohio University pointed to recent changes in Eastern Europe as evidence that unexpected political changes can happen.

Gordon Jones of DGM International stressed the importance of public policy in shaping public attitudes. Civil rights legislation, for instance, has markedly changed relationships between the races. But law can corrupt as well as inspire. Carl Anderson of the Knights of Columbus criticized several Supreme Court decisions for fostering divorce and illegitimacy. The courts do not bear sole responsibility for legal changes detrimental to family security. Steven Nock of the University of Virginia noted that in recent years state legislators have weakened many of the legal protections formerly given marriage and the family. Yet Nock believed that when legislators enacted "no fault" divorce and other new family laws, they were simply responding to a cultural shift deeper than the law. Sociologist William Donohue of LaRoche College blamed much of the decay in family life on the emergence in the 1960's of a new cultural definition of freedom, a definition in which liberty is no longer balanced by responsibility. Child psychologist Craig Peery of Brigham Young University—like Nock—regarded public policy as a very limited teacher of moral values. Healthy family life, he insisted, depends upon conscience, an innate ability to distinguish right from wrong, an ability wise parents will cultivate in their children. Sociologist Viktor Gecas of Washington State University concurred that only conscience would permit children to be released from external control. But in Gecas' opinion, even Americans with a healthy conscience face a tremendous challenge in keeping a family together. In contemporary America, divorce is no mystery. Rather than ask, What is causing family disintegration?, Gecas thought it made more sense to look for the relatively fewer answers to a different question: What features of contemporary American society encourage stability and continuity in the family?

If this volume helps readers recognize the urgency of Professor Gecas' question, it will have served its purpose.

—*Bryce J. Christensen*
Rockford, Illinois
April 1990

ENDNOTE

[1]U.S. Bureau of the Census, *Historical Statistics of the United States, Colonial Times to 1970*, Bicentennial Edition, Part 1 (Washington, D.C.: U.S. Government Printing Office, 1975), Series B214-215, B216-220, B28-35; U.S. Bureau of the Census, *Statistical Abstract of the United States: 1989*, 109th ed. (Washington, D.C.: U.S. Government Printing Office, 1989), Tables 5, 93, 127; James Witte and Herbert Lahmann, "Formation and Dissolution of One-Person Households in the United States and West Germany," *Sociology and Social Research* 73 (1988): 31-42.

The Long-Term Economic Effects of Family Dissolution

by Sara S. McLanahan

Introduction

Families headed by nonmarried women have become increasingly common during the past three decades. Whereas in 1960 less than 7 percent of all children in the United States were living in a mother-only family, by 1985 the proportion was over 21 percent.[1] Indeed, if present trends continue, over half of all children born in the past decade will live in a mother-only family at some point before reaching age 18.

Given the importance of the family as the primary social institution for raising children, it is not surprising that researchers as well as policymakers have responded to recent changes in family structure with interest and concern. Some commentators view the mother-only family as an indicator of social disorganization, signaling the demise of the family. Others regard it as an alternative family form consistent with the emerging economic independence of women. Regardless of how one views the change, the mother-only family has become a common phenomenon that promises to alter the social and economic context of family life for future generations of Americans.

This essay addresses three aspects of mother-only families: their economic well-being, their long-term economic consequences for children, and their social-policy implications. I begin by examining the economic conditions of mother-only families and discussing the proximate causes of the higher poverty rates in such families. Next I review the empirical evidence on the long-term consequences of family disruption for children and discuss different explanations for why children from nonintact families are less successful as adults than children from intact families. Finally, I discuss the ways in which the State might intervene on behalf of children either to reduce the prevalence of mother-only families or to attenuate some of the more harmful aspects of single parenthood.

The Economic Status of Mother-Only Families

Mother-only families and two-parent families differ in a number of important respects, including economic well-being, levels of stress, and social integration. The most striking of these is the difference in economic status. Roughly one of two single mothers was living below the poverty line in 1985 as compared with one in ten married couples with children.[2]

Not only are mother-only families more likely to be poor than other families, their economic status has actually deteriorated during the past two decades relative to that of other demographic groups. Figure 1 reports trends in poverty rates for three types of households: households headed by single mothers, households headed by married couples with children, and households headed by elderly persons. Between 1967 and 1985, mother-only families were the poorest of these three groups, and their relative position vis-à-vis the elderly declined dramatically. Note that the poverty rate of mother-only families was about the same in 1985 as it was in 1967, having fallen during the seventies, risen sharply in the early eighties, and fallen again after 1983.

Although many of the single mothers who live below the poverty line were poor prior to becoming parents or prior to divorce, a sizable majority are poor as a consequence of marital disruption or a nonmarital birth. Duncan and Hoffman estimate that in the year following marital dissolution the household income of divorced women is only 67 percent of their predivorce income, whereas the income of divorced men is about 90 percent of predivorce income. This indicates that marital disruption contributes directly to the poverty of mother-only families.[3]

Why are mother-only families so poor? Is the poverty of these families due to the characteristics of the parents themselves or to the failure of our social institutions to provide adequate support? In our study of the sources of income in mother-only and two-parent families, my colleague, Irwin Garfinkel, and I concluded that the proximate determinants of low income in mother-only families are (1) the low earnings capacity of the mothers, (2) the absence of child support or other economic contributions from the fathers, and (3) the meager benefits provided by the State (see table 1). While these categories do not explain the underlying causes of poverty, they are useful in identifying the areas where social policy might intervene to reduce poverty and economic insecurity.

Low Earnings Capacity

In most families with children, the earnings of the household head constitute the major source of income. Mother-only families are no different from married couple families in this respect. Thus, a mother's earnings capacity is the single most important factor in determining her family's economic status. Unfortunately, single mothers earn, on average, only about one-third as much as married fathers, partly because they have a lower hourly wage and partly because they work fewer hours.

With respect to hourly wages, the low earnings capacity of single mothers reflects the more general problem of women's low wage rates. Numerous studies have shown that women who work full time, year round earn only about 60 percent as much as full-time male workers. They also show that the wage gap has not changed very much during the past thirty years, despite women's increased participation in the labor force.[4] Thus, even if single mothers worked full time year round, their earnings would be substantially lower than those of male heads of households.

Most single mothers, however, do not work full time, and this is another source of their poverty and low income. In 1983, between 30 and 40 percent of single mothers reported no earnings at all, and of those who worked outside the home, many worked less than full time. Part of the difference in work hours between single mothers and male household heads is due to the cost of child care. Whereas in two-parent families the parents can arrange their schedules so that one parent provides child care while the other is working, the single mother rarely has such support. Thus she is doubly disadvantaged with respect to her earnings capacity: her wage rate is lower than that of the major breadwinner in a two-parent family, and her child care costs are higher.

Lack of Child Support

A second source of the income insecurity in mother-only families is the lack of child support paid by the nonresidential father. According to table 1, child support and alimony payments account for only 10 percent of the income of white single mothers and for only 3.5 percent of the income of black single mothers. While we would expect the contribution of nonresidential fathers to be lower than that of fathers in two-parent families, these figures suggest that the current level is grossly inadequate. Single mothers are bearing

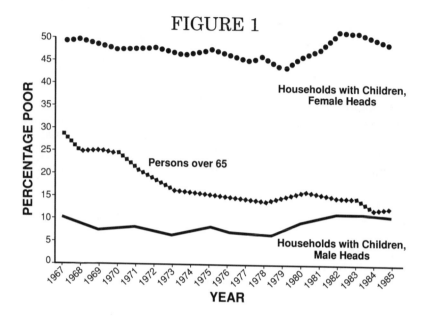

FIGURE 1

TABLE 1

Average Income Receipts of Two-Parent and
Mother-Only Families in 1982, By Race

	WHITE		BLACK	
	Married Couple Families	Mother-Only Families	Married Couple Families	Mother-Only Families
Total Cash Income	30,814	12,628	23,913	9,128
Head's Earned Income	21,932	7,666	13,508	5,363
Others' Earnings	6,377	928	8,096	827
Alimony and Child Support	227	1,246	253	322
Social Security, Pensions, Other Unearned	2,171	1,782	1,720	907
Public Assistance and Food Stamps	174	1,399	1,838	2,573

Source: Garfinkel and McLanahan, Single Mothers and Their
Children, (1986).

most of the economic costs of children alone.

The meager contribution of child support to the total family income of mother-only families is a testament of the failure of the private child support system in the United States. National data on child support awards indicate that in 1983 only about 60 percent of single mothers with children under 21 years old had a child support award. Of these, only 50 percent received full payment, 26 percent received partial payment, and 24 percent received no payment at all.[5] Even when nonresidential fathers pay support, the amount is generally low, and the value declines over time since awards are rarely indexed to the cost of living. In effect, a divorce between the two spouses in the United States often means a divorce between the father and his children.

Meager Welfare Benefits

Not only is the private child support system inadequate in providing economic support for children in mother-only families, the public child support system provides meager benefits as well. The two major programs in the public domain for aiding mother-only families are Aid to Families with Dependent Children (AFDC) and Survivors Insurance (SI). In 1983, these two programs accounted for between 15 and 25 percent of the income of white and black mother-only families, respectively. Welfare, as AFDC is usually called, is available to poor single mothers and the average benefit is quite low. Survivors Insurance is much more generous, but it is only available to widowed mothers. Since only a small proportion of single mothers are widows, AFDC is the only government program that is potentially available to most mother-only families.[6]

The AFDC program has many serious problems which contribute to its failure to reduce poverty and economic insecurity. First and most important, AFDC is available only to poor families and does nothing to help mothers and children who experience economic hardships, but do not meet the income test for welfare. Next, because the AFDC benefit is not indexed to inflation, its value falls in real terms every year if states fail to enact increases in benefits.[7] Moreover, the fact that eligibility for AFDC also entitles mother-only families to Medicaid constitutes a serious disincentive to becoming independent of welfare because the kinds of jobs available to most welfare mothers do not usually carry health insurance. Finally, by drastically reducing benefits as earnings increase, welfare programs carry with them a high tax rate which discourages employment. Thus, the choice facing poor single mothers is not an attractive one: become dependent on welfare or work full time to achieve, at best, a marginally better economic position and risk losing valuable in-kind benefits such as Medicaid and public housing.

In sum, mother-only families are much more likely to experience poverty and economic insecurity than two-parent families, and neither our public nor private child-support institutions appear to be adequate in dealing with these problems. In the next section of the paper, I examine some of the long-term consequences for children of growing up in a mother-only family and, in particular, of growing up in a poor mother-only family.

The Long-Term Consequences for Children

What are the long-term social and economic costs of family disruption for children? What is it about mother-only families that reduces the life chances of children? The answers to these questions have long been of interest to academics as well as policymakers, and the interpretation of the empirical research in this area has undergone several transformations during the past three decades. During the 1950's and most of the 1960's, the prevailing view was that divorce and out-of-wedlock births were indicative of family pathology and that children raised in such families would exhibit similar pathologies.[8] In a much publicized report on the black family, Senator Daniel Patrick Moynihan argued that the growth of female-headed families was partly responsible for the lower socioeconomic mobility of black children, and he warned that such a family structure could result in the perpetuation of a culture of poverty across generations.[9] The "Moynihan Report" stimulated a great deal of controversy at the time it was published which, in turn, led many liberal researchers to back away from the topic of family structure lest they appear racist and insensitive to the problems faced by black families.

In the early 1970's, the ideology surrounding mother-only families began to change, as evidenced by Herzog and Sudia's lengthy review of the research on children in "fatherless families." The authors challenged earlier interpretations of the relationship between family structure and children's well-being and showed that existing studies of mother-only families contained serious methodological flaws. In particular, they argued that many of the differences between mother-only and two-parent families could be explained by differences in family socioeconomic status as opposed to differences in culture or personality traits. Whereas cultural explanations were seen as "blaming the victim" for the consequences of family breakdown, economic explanations were viewed as blaming social institutions.

The Herzog and Sudia review offered a new perspective on single motherhood which, together with a changed political climate that treated black families and nonmarried mothers of all races more positively, stimulated new studies focusing on the "strengths" of mother-only families and the ways in which single mothers successfully coped with poverty and stress. While Herzog and Sudia asserted that father absence *did* have some negative consequences for children even after income was taken into account, their methodological critique was taken by many as evidence that differences between one- and two-parent families were minimal or due entirely to differences in economic status. Interestingly, the shift in consciousness during the late sixties and throughout the 1970's coincided with and served to legitimate the dramatic increase in divorce and out-of-wedlock births that occurred during this same period.

Since the late seventies, the academic community has moved beyond the rather simplistic pathological and idealizing perspectives, and a number of researchers have begun once again to examine the consequences of divorce with a more critical eye. The recent work includes studies based on large, nationally representative surveys, many of which have longitudinal designs. In addition to examining the immediate effects of divorce on children, these studies look at the long-term consequences of single parenthood and stepparent families by following children through late adolescence and into adulthood.

Recent Empirical Evidence
The new research on the intergenerational consequences of family disruption indicates that children who grow up in nonintact families are disadvantaged not only during childhood, but during adolescence and young adulthood as well. Moreover, the negative consequences associated with family structure extend across a wide range of outcomes many of which are directly associated with

long-term economic instability and dependence. We know, for example, that children from mother-only families are more likely to drop out of high school and less likely to attend college than children from intact families.[10] Not surprisingly, these children have lower earnings in adulthood and are more likely to experience unemployment and poverty than children from intact families.[11]

Children from mother-only families are also disadvantaged with respect to the formation of their own families. They are more likely to marry and have babies while in their teens, and they are more likely to have babies out of wedlock than children from two-parent families.[12] Moreover, those who marry are more likely to divorce.[13] Consequently, daughters who grow up in mother-only families are at greater risk of becoming single mothers themselves and of having to rely on welfare for their economic support than daughters who grow up with both natural parents. Finally, offspring from mother-only families are more likely to commit delinquent behavior than offspring from two-parent families.[14]

The effects of family disruption appear to be constant across a variety of racial and ethnic groups. Recent studies have shown that family disruption is associated with lower attainment among whites, blacks, Mexican Americans, Puerto Ricans, Cubans, and Native Americans. The immediate effect of divorce, or what is generally called the "stress effect," appears to be similar across racial groups, but the cumulative effect of living in a mother-only family is more negative for whites than for nonwhites. For example, whereas parents' divorce between the ages 14 and 17 has an equally negative effect on high-school graduation for whites and minorities, living in a mother-only family prior to age 14 has a stronger negative effect on whites' graduation than on nonwhites' graduation.[15] The racial difference could be due to the fact that institutional supports for single mothers are stronger in minority communities, or it could be due to the fact that minority two-parent families are exposed to more stress than white two-parent families. Either way, family structure appears to be somewhat less important in determining the life chances of minority youth than of white youth.

In addition to documenting the relationship between family structure and children's long-term welfare, the recent research on divorce and single parenthood contains a number of interesting findings about the characteristics of intact and nonintact families. We have found, for example, that the demographic characteristics of the mothers and children do not matter very much. For example, children of widowed mothers are just as likely to give birth out of wedlock as children from divorced, separated, and never-married mothers.[16] Nor does the sex of the child or the residential parent appear to make much difference. Boys and girls from mother-only families are both at greater risk of dropping out of school and starting families earlier than adolescents in two-parent families, and daughters living with single fathers are just as likely to give birth out of wedlock as daughters living with single mothers.[17]

Fourth, remarriage does *not* reduce many of the disadvantages associated with family breakup, even though step-families have more income than single-parent families. In fact, when income is taken into account, children living with stepparents appear to be even more disadvantaged than children living with single parents. Whether this is due to a lack of commitment on the part of the stepparent or whether it is because the child rejects the stepparent is not clear at this point. But the evidence that remarriage itself may cause additional problems has important policy implications. Finally, family disruptions that occur in adolescence seem to have the same consequences as disruptions occurring in early childhood, though perhaps for somewhat different reasons. Early disruptions increase the risk of long-term exposure to single parenthood and economic deprivation, whereas disruptions in adolescence interfere with parental authority at a time when parents need to be exercising a good deal of guidance and social control.

Explaining the Effects of Family Disruption

The studies described above show a positive correlation between family stability and children's long-term socioeconomic attainment. However, they do not establish that family instability *causes* lower attainment. One might argue, for example, that the lower attainment of children from divorced families is due entirely to conditions predating the dissolution of parents' union. If this were true, the children from nonintact families would be expected to be worse off than children from two-parent families *even* if their parents had remained together. In fact, they might have been worse off. This argument, which is called the selection hypothesis, assumes that pre-disruption conditions in the household were, from the child's point of view, as bad as or worse than post-disruption conditions. If this were true of all marital disruptions and nonmarriages, we would still be concerned about the welfare of the children in such families, but not about the parents' decision to live separately.

Assuming that at least some marital disruptions occur in households where the father and child have a good relationship and where the fathers invest time and money in the children, what evidence do we have that a divorce itself reduces children's well-being? In such families, wouldn't both parents continue to love and support their children after a divorce, and wouldn't the children benefit from less conflict between the parents and more parental satisfaction?

Apparently children do not always think so. In their new book, *Second Chances*, Judith Wallerstein and Sandra Blakely report that children in conflict-ridden families were angry and disappointed to learn that their parents were getting a divorce. Even ten years after the divorce, many of the offspring in their sample still resented their parents' decision and felt they had lost something very precious because of the divorce. Of course, this study is about children's perceptions of divorce as opposed to the actual effects of divorce, but nonetheless it tells us something valuable about the child's point of view.

Apart from children's perceptions, there are theoretical as well as empirical reasons for believing that divorce itself causes changes in the family that lead to negative consequences for children. Perhaps the most important change after a divorce is the decline in parents' economic investment in children.[18] In part, this is due to a loss of economies of scale: parents' income must support two households instead of one. In part, it is due to the fact that the costs of children are higher and the benefits lower for the parent who lives apart from his or her child.[19]

Divorce also alters the quantity and quality of the time parents spend with their children. The quantity of time with the nonresidential parent declines because of increases in transportation costs and the costs associated with interacting with the residential parent, and time with the residential parent declines because single mothers must increase the number of hours they work in order to compensate for the loss of income. The quality of parent-child relations is affected by the fact that parents are under a considerable amount of stress during the first year after a separation or divorce and also by the fact that parental conflict over child support and custody rights may continue for many years. Stress and parental conflict undermine parental authority and interfere with children's internalization of parental role models and parental values. Socialization theory suggests that such disjunctions have negative consequences for cognitive and emotional development.[20]

Finally, divorce affects the quality of children's community resources and peer relationships. Divorce increases the likelihood that a child will live in a disadvantaged community where jobs are scarce, school quality is poor, and social networks are weak. Since the payoffs from completing high school and delaying parenthood are lower in such communities, adolescents are less likely to stay in school and more likely to become teen parents. In addition, disorganized communities are less able to exercise social control and therefore children are more likely to engage in deviant activities that may undermine school performance and commitment. Even for children living in middle- or working-class neighborhoods, divorce may interrupt community ties and promote membership in deviant subgroups. Residential mobility is much higher in recently divorced families than in stable families, which means that a substantial proportion of children from newly divorced families must adjust to new schools and make new friends at the same time they are trying to deal with a change in economic status and separation from their parent.[21] When parents are under considerable stress, teenagers are likely to turn to peers for support. The latter strategy can be positive or negative, depending on the culture of the peer group. Unfortunately, children from divorced families are more likely to feel deviant themselves and therefore they are likely to identify with a deviant subgroup.

My colleagues and I at the University of Wisconsin have been testing many of these ideas about why children from nonintact families have lower socioeconomic attainment than children from intact families. While much of this research is still in progress and while the evidence is not always consistent across different studies, several patterns are beginning to emerge. First, the most consistent finding is that income is a crucial factor in predicting children's long-term attainment. Differences in family income account for between 25 and 50 percent of the difference in high school graduation between children from intact and nonintact families and for about 25 percent of the difference in outcomes such as teen marriage or premarital birth. These percentages probably underestimate the true effect of income differences since none of the studies thus far have measured differences in family wealth.

Aside from income, we have learned a few things about the kinds of parenting practices and community characteristics that enhance children's attainment and how these are likely to change as a consequence of family disruption. We know, for example, that single parents and stepparents are less likely to monitor their children's school work and social life and that stepparents are less likely to hold high educational expectations for their children than parents in intact families.[22] We also know that children living with single mothers are more likely to live in disadvantaged neighborhoods, to attend poor quality schools, and to associate with deviant subgroups than children living with both parents.[23] Unfortunately, we have not been able to demonstrate that these differences *account for* the contrast in school achievement and family behavior between children from intact and nonintact families, but this may be due to the fact that our measures of socialization practices and community quality are rather crude. Most importantly perhaps, we have not been able to rule out the selection hypothesis which argues that the negative consequences associated with growing up in nonintact families are due to factors that predate the divorce or nonmarital birth. Some progress has been made in this area, however. For example, we know that inherited ability does not account for differences in the educational attainment of children from intact and nonintact families.[24] We also know that *changes* in family structure (going from a two-parent household to a one-parent household) lead to *changes* in parental practices, neighborhood conditions, and school behavior.[25] The latter is important because the analysis of change scores allows us to control for some of the pre-divorce family effects. Finally, we have used statistical techniques to control for unobserved differences between intact and nonintact families and have found that family structure effects persist even after making these adjustments. Thus, while we are fairly confident that divorce itself has some negative consequences for children, we do not have a good estimate of the magnitude of this effect.

Policy Implications

What are the social-policy implications of the research on the intergenerational consequences of divorce? Should the State outlaw divorce for couples with children? Should it make marital dissolution more difficult to obtain by narrowing the grounds for divorce or changing the tax code to penalize parents who live apart from their children? Before these questions can be answered, both the costs and benefits of preventing divorce must be weighed.

Clearly, the costs of such an action are very high. Outlawing divorce would impose major restrictions on individual freedom and would expose women and children who live in abusive situations to considerable harm. The benefits are more difficult to evaluate. Eliminating divorce would raise the national high school graduation rate from its present level, which is about 86 percent, to 88 percent—not a very large increase. The reason the aggregate effect is so small is that dropping out of high school is a rare event that affects only a small percentage of the population. If it becomes more common, the effect would be larger.

Consider nonmarital births among young black women. If the parents of these young women had married and remained married, the proportion of their daughters who gave birth out of wedlock would have been 43 percent instead of 55—a substantial reduction. Premarital births are more common among black women than dropping out of school, and therefore the effect of family disruption is larger at the aggregate level.

While the potential for reducing premarital births is sizable, these numbers must be viewed as an upper-bound estimate of the effect of divorce. Both sets of estimates assume that couples who decide not to marry or not to stay married are just as good parents as those who remain together, which is clearly too strong an assumption given our current level of knowledge. In short, until the selectivity issue is resolved, we cannot be sure about the size of the benefit that would result from increased restrictions on divorce.

While outlawing divorce and requiring marriage are probably not justifiable, less draconian measures may be in order. The research described above indicates that as much as half of the disadvantage associated with living in a mother-only family is due to differences in family income. Increasing the income and economic stability of single mothers would go a long way toward reducing the disadvantages of their children.

As noted in the first section of the paper, single mothers have three major sources of income: own earnings, child support from nonresidential fathers, and public transfers from the State. Not surprisingly, current policies for reducing poverty in mother-only families address all three sources of income.

Increasing Mothers' Earnings

Policies aimed at increasing mothers' earnings include affirmative action, occupational desegregation, comparable worth, and child care. Most analysts agree that some of the difference in the male-female wage differential is due to discrimination, either inside or outside the labor market. Affirmative action and job desegregation policies are designed to reduce discrimination and increase women's access to higher–paying jobs. Comparable worth is designed to increase the wages of persons in female-dominated jobs (mostly women, by definition). Both policies would improve the economic status of single mothers, and pay equity in particular would have a strong impact on poor single mothers.

Subsidizing child care is another way to raise the economic status of single mothers. As noted earlier, a large proportion of single mothers do not work full time because the cost of paid child care is high and because they cannot arrange for free child care. Public provision of such care would allow these mothers to work more hours and would increase earnings and family income.

At present, the government has two different mechanisms for providing child care. For families in the lower half of the income distribution, there are income-tested child care subsidies, which cost less than 2 billion dollars per year. For middle- and upper-middle-income families, there is the child care tax credit in the federal income tax, which costs over 3.5 billion dollars.[26]

One solution is to combine the two mechanisms into a single program which provides a refundable tax credit for those with very low earnings and a declining tax credit for those with higher earnings. An alternative would be to provide child care for all families and to charge a sliding-scale fee based upon income. Either of these two strategies would target more child-care dollars to poor single mothers than the present system.

Increasing Child-Support Transfers

Policies designed to increase the child support paid by nonresidential fathers include proposals to strengthen paternity enforcement and insure that all children with a living absent parent have a child-support award, proposals to standardize the amount of the award so that benefits increase as the father's income increases, and proposals to improve the collection of child-support obligations.[27]

How much can we expect of child-support reform? To what extent can increases in support payments reduce poverty and income insecurity in mother-only families? Some argue that shifting some of the economic burden from mothers to fathers will reduce the economic well-being of nonresidential fathers and push their new families into poverty. While most fathers will certainly have less disposable income and while some fathers may be forced into poverty, the evidence suggests this will not occur in the majority of cases.[28] First, as noted earlier, studies of the economic consequences of divorce show that the income loss experienced by single mothers is much greater than the loss experienced by nonresidential fathers. Moreover, estimates of absent fathers' ability to pay indicate that their average income is about $19,000 per year, only $3,000 less than the average for all prime-age males.[29] Estimates of the potential benefits from establishing a uniform standard and collecting the total amount owed indicate that child support reform would reduce poverty rates by 7 percentage points (from 39 percent to 32 percent) and would reduce the poverty gap by about 31 percent.[30]

Increasing Public Transfers

A final way of aiding single mothers and their children is to change welfare policy. In recent years welfare (AFDC) has come under considerable attack, and some analysts and policymakers feel that the program does more harm than good. A major criticism of the system is that it discourages single mothers from entering the labor force by imposing a high tax rate on earnings. As noted above, welfare recipients lose nearly a dollar in benefits for each dollar earned. They also lose health care and other income-tested benefits if their earnings increase too much. Given the high tax rate, their low earnings capacity, and the costs of child care, many single mothers would be worse off working full time than they are depending on welfare.

In response to these concerns, many critics have called for replacing welfare with work. While such concerns date back at least to the early 1960's, the past few years have seen a resurgence of interest and bipartisan support for strengthening work requirements. Many states are experimenting with different versions of work and training programs, and others are planning to do so. The new Family Support Act requires all states to establish work-welfare programs for mothers with children over 6 years old. Included under the "work-welfare" rubric are a broad range of programs which differ greatly in their intent and implementation. While some programs simply impose a work requirement on the mother in exchange for her welfare check, many are aimed at providing resources that facilitate work, e.g., child care, transportation, training, and education.[31] To date the evidence suggests that some states are spending a good deal of money on training and education, money that probably would not have been spent in the absence of a change in expectations regarding work.

The Tradeoff Between Prevalence and Economic Well-Being

The policies described above would clearly reduce poverty and economic insecurity in mother-only families. They would also impose social costs. Insofar as they are successful, the reforms will encourage more women to divorce and become single parents. Thus, while children in mother-only families will be better off than they were in times past, more children will be exposed to single parenthood. How should we evaluate the tradeoff between increasing the economic well-being of single mothers and their children and reducing the prevalence of mother-only families? Some would argue that prevalence is not a concern, that it is poverty rather than single motherhood that is a problem. If income were the only cause of the relative disadvantage of children from nonintact families, this argument might be convincing, although there would still be the question of society's willingness to subsidize single-parent households enough to eliminate their economic disadvantage. Unfortunately, the recent research indicates that income is *not* the only source of disadvantage in mother-only families.

To evaluate the tradeoff between the benefits of reducing economic hardship and the costs of increasing prevalence, we need information not only on the intergenerational consequences of growing up in mother-only families (net of selection into that status), but also on the effect of income on marital disruption and nonmarriage. Such information is not available at this time.

The policies aimed at reducing poverty and income insecurity have other tradeoffs as well. The thrust of both the child-care proposals and the welfare-reform initiatives is to increase the income in mother-only families by increasing the labor-force participation of single mothers. Thus, whereas the new system provides children with more income, it reduces the amount of time they can spend with their mothers. Will the gain in income be offset by the loss in mothers' time?

The answer is: it depends. Research on mothers' employment and day care generally indicates that children of working mothers do just as well as children of nonworking mothers and that, except for the very youngest children, day care has no negative consequences.[32] These results must be viewed with caution, however. All of the studies of maternal employment are based on women who work voluntarily. For example, the benefits observed in studies of work-welfare programs are based on mothers whose participation in the programs was voluntary, and therefore the results cannot be generalized to all welfare mothers. Second, research on the effects of day care on children indicates that the *quality* of care is what determines the effect on children. Therefore, to evaluate the trade-off between income and mother's time we need to know about the type of care that children will receive in the future. If that care is poor, the long-term social and economic costs to society may be greater than the gains.

Conclusions

Until recently, many analysts as well as lay persons believed that divorce had no negative consequences for children, beyond the temporary stress associated with family disruption. This belief emerged during the 1970's, when divorce rates were at their peak, and served to legitimate the new ideology that children's interests are best served when their parents pursue their own personal welfare. During the past several years, a number of studies based on large, nationally representative surveys have challenged this view by showing that divorce has long-term negative economic consequences for children.

While there is no definitive proof that divorce *causes* lower attainment in children, there are good theoretical reasons for believing that it reduces the quantity and quality of parental investment, which in turn may reduce children's well-being. The most important loss that accompanies divorce, and the loss that is most strongly associated with negative outcomes in children, is economic insecurity and income deprivation. The financial contribution from the nonresidential parent (usually the father) drops dramatically after the parents break up, and the residential parent (usually the mother) is rarely able to compensate for the income loss. Consequently, children in mother-only families have fewer resources to draw on while they are growing up, and their opportunity for mobility is lower than it would have been if the parents had remained together.

What, if anything, can society do to reduce the negative consequences of divorce for children? At least three possible answers to this question come to mind: we can try to reduce the incidence of divorce by tightening divorce laws and changing the tax code to make divorce more costly for parents; we can try to increase mothers' earnings by reducing labor market discrimination and subsidizing child care; and we can strengthen both our private and public child support systems. The first strategy is preventive; the second and third are designed to address the major cause of the long-term negative consequences of divorce — poverty and economic insecurity. All of these strategies have costs.

Restricting divorce means reducing personal freedom, a value that is strongly embedded in American culture. Increasing family income through mothers' employment means reducing the time children spend with their mothers and increasing women's economic independence, which in turn contributes to higher female headship rates in the future. Reforming child support means both intruding on the private life of nonresidential fathers (in behalf of mothers and children) and increasing the public obligation for children. The former imposes costs on individual freedom, and the latter imposes economic costs on society.

—Sara S. McLanahan is professor of sociology at the University of Wisconsin at Madison.

ENDNOTES

[1]U.S. Bureau of the Census, *Current Population Reports*, Series P-20, nos. 105 (1960), 106 (1961), and 423 (1988), Washington, D.C.: United States Government Printing Office.

[2]Unless otherwise indicated, the information reported in this section of the paper is taken from Irwin Garfinkel and Sara S. McLanahan, *Single Mothers and Their Children: A New American Dilemma* (Washington, D.C.: Urban Institute, 1986).

[3]For additional estimates of the income loss associated with divorce, see Lenore Weitzman, *The Divorce Revolution* (New York: The Free Press, 1985). Mary Jo Bane has shown that the relationship between marital disruption and poverty is quite different for blacks and whites. For whites, about 75 percent of new poverty cases among single mothers are due to marital disruption, whereas 25 percent of the cases are "reshuffled poverty," e.g. an unmarried daughter from a poor family has a child and becomes a female household head or a poor married woman gets a divorce and establishes an independent household. For blacks, the percentages are reversed, about 35 percent of new poverty cases are "event caused poverty," whereas 65 percent are "reshuffled poverty." Mary Jo Bane, "Household composition and poverty," pp. 209-31 in S.H. Danziger and D.H. Weinberg, eds., *Fighting Poverty: What Works and What Doesn't* (Cambridge: Harvard University Press, 1986).

[4]Recent studies indicate that since 1980 the gender wage gap has been narrowing. Francine Blau and Andrea Beller, "Trends in earnings differentials by gender, 1971-87," *Industrial Relations Review*, July 1988, pp. 5133-39; and also Morley Gunderson, "Male-female wage differentials and policy responses," *Journal of Economic Literature* 27 (March 1989): 46-72.

[5]Garfinkel and McLanahan, *Single Mothers and Their Children*, 1986.

[6]Single mothers also received food stamps, Medicaid, and housing benefits. Food stamps account for about 3 percent of the total income of white mother-only families and for about 8.6 percent of the total income of black mother-only families. Garfinkel and McLanahan, *Single Mothers and Their Children*, 1986.

[7]Welfare benefits declined by 13 percent between 1975 and 1980 because benefit levels were not indexed to inflation. Budget cuts and low inflation contributed to another 12 percent decline in benefits between 1970 and 1980. Garfinkel and McLanahan, *Single Mothers and Their Children*, 1986.

[8]Much of the research at this time was based on highly selective samples, such as children in treatment for psychological disorders or wards of the criminal justice system. Thus it is not surprising that personal failures rather than social factors were used to account for differences associated with family structure.

[9]Daniel P. Moynihan. *The Negro Family: The Case for National Action* (Washington, D.C.: U.S. Department of Labor, Office of Family Planning and Research, 1965).

[10]Elizabeth Herzog and Cecilia Sudia, "Children in Fatherless Families," in B. Caldwell and H. Ricciuti, eds., *Review of Child Development Research,* Vol. 3 (Chicago: University of Chicago Press, 1973); James Coleman, "Social Capital in the Creation of Human Capital," *American Journal of Sociology* 94, Supplement 1988, pp. S95-120; Sara S. McLanahan, "Family structure and the reproduction of poverty," *American Journal of Sociology* 90 (1985): 873-901; Sheilia Krein and Andrea Beller, "Educational attainment of children from single-parent families: differences by exposure, gender, and race," *Demography* 25 (1989): 221-34; Gary Sandefur, Sara S. McLanahan, and Roger Wojtkiewicz, "The impact of race and family structure on school enrollment and high school completions," paper presented at the Population Association of America annual meeting, Baltimore, Maryland, 1989; Nan Astone and Sara McLanahan, "The effect of family structure on school completion," paper presented at the annual meeting of the Population Association of America, Baltimore, Maryland, 1989.

[11]Mary R. Corcoran, R. Gordon, D. Laren, and G. Solon, "Intergenerational transmission of education, income, and earnings," Institute of Public Policy Studies,

University of Michigan, Ann Arbor, 1987; Martha S. Hill, Sue Augustyniak, and Michael Ponza, "Effects of parental divorce on children's attainments: an empirical comparison of five hypotheses," Survey Research Institute, University of Michigan, Ann Arbor, 1989; Sara McLanahan, "Family structure and dependency," *Demography* 25 (1988): 1-16.

[12]Allen F. Abrahamse, Peter Morrison, and Linda J. Waite, "Single teen mothers: spotting susceptible adolescents in advance," paper presented at the annual meetings of the Population Association of America, Chicago, 1987; Dennis P. Hogan and Evelyn M. Kitagawa, "The impact of social status, family structure and neighborhood on the fertility of black adolescents," *American Journal of Sociology* 90 (1985): 825-55; Sara S. McLanahan and Larry Bumpass, "Intergenerational consequences of family disruption," *American Journal of Sociology* 94 (1988): 130-52; Sara S. McLanahan, Nan Astone, and Nadine Marks, "The role of mother-only families in reproducing poverty," 1990, forthcoming in *Children and Poverty*, Aletha Huston, ed., (Boston: Cambridge University Press).

[13]McLanahan and Bumpass, "Intergenerational consequences of family disruption," 1988.

[14]Ross Matsueda and Karen Heimer, "Race, family structure, and delinquency: a test of differential association and social control theories," *American Sociological Review* 52 (1987): 826-40.

[15]Gary Sandefur, Sara McLanahan, and Roger Wojtkiewicz, "The impact of race and family structure on school enrollment and high school completions," 1989.

[16]Note, however, that children who grow up with widowed mothers are more likely to graduate from high school than children from other nonintact families, Sara McLanahan, "Family structure and the reproduction of poverty," 1985.

[17]McLanahan and Bumpass, "Intergenerational consequences of family disruption," 1988.

[18]Although the discussion focuses on the effects of divorce, much of what is said is also true of families in which the parents never marry.

[19]See Weiss and Willis for a theoretical discussion of the changes in the costs of children after divorce. Yoram Weiss and Robert Willis, "Children as collective goods and divorce settlements," *Journal of Labor Economics* 3 (1985): 268-92.

[20]E. Mavis Hetherington, Martha Cox, and R. Cox, "The aftermath of divorce," in J.H. Stevens, ed., *Mother-Child, Father-Child Relations* (Washington, D.C.: National Association of the Education of Young Children, 1978); Judith Wallerstein and Sandra Blakely, *Second Chances: Men, Women and Children a Decade After Divorce*, (New York: Ticknor and Fields, 1989).

[21]Garfinkel and McLanahan, *Single Mothers and Their Children*, 1986.

[22]McLanahan, Astone, and Marks, "The role of mother-only families in reproducing poverty," 1990; Astone and McLanahan, "The effect of family structure on school completion," 1989.

[23]Sandefur *et al.*, "The impact of race and family structure on school enrollment and high school completions," 1989; Astone and McLanahan, "The effect of family structure on school completion," 1989.

[24]Sandefur *et al.*, "The impact of race and family structure on school enrollment and high school completions," 1989; Astone and McLanahan, "The effect of family structure on school completion," 1989.

[25]Sandefur *et al.*, "The impact of race and family structure on school enrollment and

high school completions,"1989; Astone and McLanahan, "The effect of family structure on school completion," 1989.

[26]Irwin Garfinkel, "The potential of child care to reduce poverty and welfare dependence," paper presented to Wingspread Symposium on the Economic Implications and Benefits of Child Care, January 24-26, 1988, Racine, Wisconsin.

[27]The Wisconsin Child Support Assurance Program adds an additional component which guarantees a minimum benefit to every child with a living absent parent. If the amount collected from the nonresidential parent falls below a certain level, the State supplements that private child support with a public benefit. See Garfinkel and McLanahan, *Single Mothers and Their Children*, 1986, for a more detailed discussion of this program.

[28]Ann Nichols-Casebolt, "The economic impact of child support reform on the poverty status of custodial and noncustodial families," *Journal of Marriage and the Family* 48 (1986): 875-880.

[29]Irwin Garfinkel and Donald Oellerich, 1989, "Noncustodial fathers' ability to pay child support," *Demography* (forthcoming).

[30]Donald Oellerich, Irwin Garfinkel, and Philip K. Robins, "Private child support: current and potential impacts," Institute for Research on Poverty Discussion Paper #888-89, University of Wisconsin, Madison, Wisconsin, 1989.

[31]Judy M. Gueron, "Work initiatives for welfare recipients: lessons from a multi-state experiment," (New York: Manpower Demonstration Research Corporation, 1986).

[32]For reviews see Barbara Heyns, "The influence of parental work on children's school achievement," in *Families That Work: Children in a Changing World*, S.B. Kamerman and C.D. Hayes, eds., (Washington, D.C.: National Academy Press, 1985) and Lois Hoffman, "Maternal Employment: 1979," *American Psychologist* 34 (1979): 859-65. A recent report indicates that maternal employment may have negative consequences for sons in middle-class families. See Lindsay Chase-Lansdale, Sonalde Desai, and Robert Michael, 1989, "The effects of child care on child development: mother or market?" *Demography* (forthcoming).

The Impact
of Family Dissolution
on the Emotional Health of
Children and Adolescents

by Armand M. Nicholi, Jr., M.D.

The primary symptom of the changes in family structure is the enormous emotional impact on children and adolescents imposed by family dissolution. Changes in the structure of the family have resulted in over one-third of children in this country under 18 growing up in a home with one or both parents missing. Over a million children a year are involved in divorce cases. Over a half million children a year are born to unmarried women, 40 percent of these to teenagers. Census data suggests the number of single-parent families is growing at twenty times the rate of two-parent families.

What difference does it make whether a child grows up with one parent absent or even both parents absent, as long as it has reasonably good food and shelter and someone to provide its basic everyday needs? Here, of course, we must consider what we know of human development and what research tells us.

If any one factor influences the character development and emotional stability of a person, it is the quality of the relationship he experiences as a child with *both* of his parents. Conversely, if people suffering from severe nonorganic emotional illness have one experience in common, it is the absence of a parent through death, divorce, time-demanding job, or absence for other reasons. A parent's inaccessibility, either physically, emotionally, or both, can exert a profound influence on the child's emotional health (Bronfenbrenner, 1974; Zwerling, 1978; Nicholi, 1980). These impressions come from a vast body of research which began over three decades ago and that led the World Health Organization over twenty years ago to make this statement: "What is believed to be essential for mental health is that the infant and young child should experience a warm, intimate, and continuous relationship with his mother. . ." (Bowlby, 1951, 1965). And more recent research has demonstrated the full emotional impact on the child of the father. What has been shown over and over again to contribute most to the emotional development of the child is a close, warm, sustained and continuous relationship with *both* parents.

A few general comments may serve as preface to a review of the literature concerning the impact of parental absence on the emotional development of the child. First, the literature covers a vast body of research that began over 40 years ago with the studies of Anna Freud and Dorothy Burlingham. Over the ensuing years, studies have been carried out throughout the world on the effects of parental absence through death, divorce, or time-demanding jobs. Thus the research has focused on both permanent absence through death and divorce — and on temporary, short-term absence brought about by hospitalization of the child (or hospitalization of the parent) or the brief absence caused by placing a child in a nursery or in a day-care center. The many recent studies of day-care centers are in large measure a study of the effects of short-term parental absence on children.

Second, this research consists of retrospective studies in which the researchers view *causal* processes of a current disorder by exploring the events and conditions of the past; in these studies, the early life experiences of adolescents or adults with disorders such as severe depression or schizophrenia are studied to see if the onset of these illnesses relates to the loss of a parent in infancy or childhood. They may also look at whether a group of patients with a particular disorder has a higher incidence of having lost a parent through death than a control group. This retrospective research method, though used widely in medical research, has limitations and is therefore complemented by prospective studies, in which a possible pathogen is identified and patients subjected to the pathogen are followed over a long period of time. If the loss of a parent, for example, is considered a possible pathogen, then researchers can follow a large group of children who lose a parent through death or divorce and observe the short- and long-term effects of the loss.

One other comment about this research. In addition to the magnitude of it, the studies taken as a whole paint an unmistakably clear picture of the adverse effects of parental absence. Yet this vast body of research is almost totally ignored by our society. Why have even the professionals tended to ignore this research? Perhaps the answer is, to put it most simply, because the findings are unacceptable. Attitudes which now prevail toward parental absence resemble those once prevalent toward cigarette smoking. For decades Americans ignored the large body of research concerning the adverse effects of cigarette smoke. We had excellent studies for decades before we began to respond to the data. Apparently as a society, we refuse to accept data that demands a radical change in our lifestyle.

Because of the vastness of this research, the discussion here will be restricted to only a few representative samples. First, the earlier studies that began with Anna Freud and Dorothy Burlingham occurred in the early 40's. These studies focused primarily on infants and children separated from their parents during the war, children observed in the Hampstead Nurseries, and children hospitalized or institutionalized (Burlingham and Freud, 1942; 1943). Although Levey in 1937, Bowlby in 1940, and Bender and Yarnell in 1944 presented empirical evidence suggesting an etiological relationship between certain forms of psychopathic personality and severely disruptive child-mother relationships, researchers had published very little data that suggested any causal relationship between psychopathology and early separation experiences. Goldfarb in 1943 and Spitz in 1946, however, carried out studies that, although different, nevertheless related to those of Burlingham and Freud. They studied infants raised in institutions without any contact with their biological parents. Spitz's classic though controversial papers on "Hospitalism" and "Anaclytic Depression" showed how the replacement of the mother with an inadequate mother substitute caused profound physical and psychological retardation and subjected these infants to an extremely high incidence of physical and psychological morbidity. Thirty-seven percent of the 90 infants studied by Spitz died within two years. A large percentage developed a syndrome he called "Anaclytic Depression," consisting of weepiness, withdrawal, agitation, insomnia, weight loss, increased susceptibility to infections, expressions of dejection and stupor.

Later studies — Robertson and Bowlby in 1952, Heinicke in 1956, and Heinicke and Westheimer in 1966 — also observed children in institutional settings separated from their parents. Most of these studies were well designed and well controlled. Many focused on brief separation from parents.

The findings of all these early studies can be summed up as follows:

The findings of all these early studies can be summed up as follows:

1. When a child is separated from his parents permanently and not provided adequate substitute care, the infant becomes visibly distressed and is subjected to high risk for both physical and psychological disturbances in development.

2. When a child is separated from its mother unwillingly even during brief periods of time, the child shows distress, and when placed in a strange environment and cared for by a succession of strange people, the distress becomes intense. The reaction follows a typical sequence. As Bowlby points out, the child at first protests vigorously and tries desperately to recover the mother. Later he seems to despair of recovering her, although he remains preoccupied with her return, and still later if she does not return, he seems to lose interest in her and to become emotionally detached from her. These early studies focused primarily on the absence of the mother and discontinuities in the early child-mother relationship. They have considerable relevance to recent trends in our society, as an increasing number of mothers with young children work and the care of the children is relegated to outside agencies.

Other studies focused on the absence of the father. Bronfenbrenner, Reikers, and others have all explored the impact of the absent father on children of different age levels. For a representative view of these studies, consider a study by Trunnel published in 1968 in the *Archives of General Psychiatry*. Trunnel studied the effect of the periodic absence of the father on 200 children seen at a military medical clinic where the father's absence was due to his military occupation. The children ranged from 3 to 18 years of age.

The researchers found early reaction to the father's departure resembled reactions to children who lose a father by death: (1) rageful protest over desertion, (2) denial of the loss and an intense fantasy relationship with the parent, (3) efforts at reunion, (4) irrational guilt and a need for punishment, (5) exaggerated sepa-

When the father left home, the child was often allowed to do things not otherwise permitted. This made it difficult for the child to internalize a consistent set of standards for controlling his behavior. In several instances, the father's leaving was followed by disobedience, decline in school performance, and aggressive anti-social behavior. The child seemed unable to control himself and this loss of control is especially interesting in light of the observation that more people today come to psychiatrists because of a lack of impulse control.

Several other recent studies bear on the absence or inaccessibility of the father and all point to the same conclusions: A father absent for long periods contributes to (a) low motivation for achievement, (b) inability to defer immediate gratification for later rewards, (c) low self-esteem, (d) susceptibility to group influence and to juvenile delinquency. The absent father tends to have passive, effeminate, dependent sons lacking in achievement, motivation, and independence. These are general findings with, of course, many exceptions (Rekers *et al.*, 1983; Rekers, 1983).

My personal interest in the impact of parental loss on emotional development and its relationship to psychopathology began in the late 1960's. From my clinical experience and from my research with college students, I began to notice (1) that a large number suffered from an incapacitating symptomatic or characterological conflict, (2) that they seemed to have in common a number of traumatic early experiences with a rejecting, inaccessible, or absent parent, and (3) when we looked at their histories carefully, there appeared to be some causal relation between the earlier experience and the emotional illness they were suffering as an adult. About 20 years ago I began studying several hundred young men who had dropped out of Harvard for psychiatric reasons. Two characteristics of the group were (1) a marked isolation and alienation from their parents, especially their fathers, and (2) an overwhelming apathy and lack of motivation. In addition, among those who had the most serious illness, that is, those hospitalized and diagnosed as schizophrenics, a large number lost one or both parents through death; when compared with several control groups, this finding proved highly significant statistically. This provided me with my first clue that there might be an association between a missing parent and emotional illness (Nicholi, 1967).

In 1979, Norman Watt and I published in the *American Journal of Orthopsychiatry* results of two large retrospective investigations demonstrating a statistically significant higher incidence of parental death in the childhood of schizophrenics compared with other psychiatric patients and with normal controls. We concluded that this high frequency of parental death implicated childhood bereavement as a contributing etiological factor in schizophrenia. We emphasized that the pathogenic influence of premature parental death in no way is specific for schizophrenia. We noted that our findings underscored the data of a large body of research demonstrating the possibly pathogenic influence on a child of a physically absent or emotionally inaccessible parent. In another study published in the *Archives of General Psychiatry* in 1982, Small and I reported findings of a study demonstrating a statistically significant higher rate of parental divorce and death within the family of children hospitalized with a diagnosis of mass hysteria. Our findings suggested that previous loss in a child's life influenced that child's vulnerability to current loss and predisposed that child to mass hysteria when involved in an epidemic of this illness.

As I became involved in my own research and as I began to gather more experience with patients clinically, I began to realize that absence through death was the most severe kind of absence. But there were many other kinds of absences that affected children. Parents could be absent because of emotional illness, because of time-demanding jobs and, more and more in our society, because of divorce. The more recent research on parental absence focuses on separation from parents as a result of divorce. The divorce rate has risen over 700 percent in this century, most of this rise occurring during the 1970's; 22 million American children (over one-third under 18) have one or both natural parents missing from their homes (U.S. Bureau of the Census, 1975, 1989; Glick, 1988).

Perhaps the most extensive and well-known study of the effects of divorce on children is Wallerstein and Kelley's five-year study of 60 divorced families published in 1980 (Wallerstein, 1980). A few findings deserve particular attention:

— The initial reaction of over 90 percent of the children was "an acute sense of shock, intense fears, and grieving which the children found overwhelming."

— Half of the children feared being abandoned forever by
   the parent who had left (a realistic fear in light of other
   studies [Jellinek and Slovik, 1981] that show that
   within three years after the divorce decree 50 percent of
   the fathers never see their children). One-third feared
   being abandoned by the custodial parent. The children
   were preoccupied with the fear of waking to find both
   parents gone.

— Following the divorce a significant number of children
   suffered feelings of despondency, rejection, anger, and
   guilt. The researchers report: "Two-thirds of the
   children, especially the younger children, yearned for
   the absent parent . . . with an intensity we found
   profoundly moving."

— Five years after the divorce 37 percent of the children
   were moderately to severely depressed, were intensely
   unhappy and dissatisfied with their lives, and their
   unhappiness was greater at five years than it had been
   at one and a half years after the divorce.

— Ten years after the divorce 41 percent of the children
   were doing poorly; "they were entering adulthood as
   worried, underachieving, self-deprecating, and
   sometimes angry young men and women. The rest were
   strikingly uneven in how they adjusted to the world; it
   is too early to say how they will turn out." Some of these
   children, especially the girls, did not show any
   symptoms until they were about to enter a close
   relationship themselves as young adults. At this time
   they experienced fears, anxieties, guilt and concerns
   that had apparently been suppressed over the years.
   The investigators found that 66 percent of the young
   women between the ages of 19 and 23 were seriously
   derailed many years after they experienced the divorce
   as a young child. The investigators concluded, "We can
   no longer say — as most experts have held in recent
   years — that girls are generally less troubled by the
   divorce experience than boys. Our study strongly

indicates for the first time that girls experience serious
effects of divorce at the time they are entering young
adulthood. Perhaps the risk for boys and girls is
equalized over the long term."

The investigators found that adolescents appeared to be particularly vulnerable to the effects of divorce. This is in marked
contrast to parents who feel that because the children are no longer
small they will not be affected by divorce. Adolescents in this study
spoke again and again of how much they needed a family structure,
how much they wanted to be protected, and how much they yearned
for "clear guidelines for moral behavior." The investigators found
that as these children grew older, their own families appeared
particularly vulnerable to divorce.

Other studies have found that children of divorce make up an
estimated 60 percent of child patients in clinical treatment and 80
to 100 percent of adolescents in in-patient mental hospital settings.

These investigators found that children — "especially boys and
young men — continue to need their fathers after divorce and
suffered feelings of rejection even when they were visited regularly."
This finding is especially meaningful in light of studies that show
that three years after divorce 50 percent of the fathers never see
their children again (Wallerstein, 1980, 1989; Jellinek and Slovik,
1981).

A vast body of research compiled during the past several decades,
beginning with Anna Freud's and Dorothy Burlingham's (1942)
work in London, has demonstrated that the absence of a parent
through death, divorce, or a time-demanding job contributes to the
many forms of emotional disorder, especially the anger, rebel-
liousness, low self-esteem, depression, and antisocial behavior that
characterize those adolescents who take drugs, become pregnant
out of wedlock, or commit suicide (Wallerstein, 1980; Jellinek and
Slovik, 1981; Goldney, 1982; Davis, 1983; Nicholi, 1983, 1985).

Statistics show over a million teenage pregnancies per year,
with over a quarter of a million terminating in abortion. That 50
percent of teenage marriages end in divorce within five years
makes these findings no less disturbing. The rate for births to
unmarried versus married teenagers increased 76 percent during
the past 20 years and far surpasses the rate in England, France,
Sweden, or the Netherlands. Studies indicate that changes in the

American family, especially an absent parent, contribute significantly to this increase (Baldwin, 1982; Levy and Grinker, 1983). Deutsch points out that teenage pregnancies are "compulsive" and that sexual instruction and modern contraceptives will do little to prevent them.

Between the years 1960 and 1980, the suicide rate among adolescents in the United States increased 150 percent (Deykin, 1986). In some American cities, the increase has been even more dramatic. In one city, for example, in the four years between 1976 and 1980, completed suicides among 10 to 14 year olds increased 80 percent and in 15 to 19 year olds increased 100 percent (Shafii *et al.*, 1985). Authorities now refer to the explosive increase in adolescent suicide during the seventh and eighth decades of this century as a "national tragedy" (Davis, 1983; Deykin, 1986). Suicide ranks as the third leading cause of death among adolescents in the United States (after accidents and homicides). Although thousands of adolescents take their lives each year, researchers emphasize that a large percentage of suicides — because of stigma and guilt experienced by the family — go unreported. Families often tend to report death by suicide as death by accident. Researchers further estimate that for every adolescent who succeeds in committing suicide, another 50 to 100 attempt it (Rosenkrantz, 1978; Peck, 1981).

The rapid increase in the rate of suicide over a relatively short period of time appears to be limited to children and adolescents — the rate of suicide among older age groups has actually decreased or remained stable. The rate of increase has also remained relatively stable in adolescent women, the increase occurring primarily in white adolescent men. Although adolescent men outnumber women in completed suicides, about four or five to one, adolescent women outnumber men by about the same margin in number of attempts (Frederick, 1985). In 1982 among white men between the ages of 15 and 24, 21.2 per 100,000 population completed suicides, with a rate of 4.5 for white women.

What causes this incredible number of children and adolescents to kill themselves? Though all human behavior is complex and multidetermined, an overview of recent research in the field points — with unmistakable clarity — to the changes in child-rearing practices and in the stability of the home as significant factors in the rapidly rising rate of suicide. First, the increase in suicide multidetermined, an overview of recent research in the field points — with unmistakable clarity — to the changes in child-rearing practices and in the stability of the home as significant factors in the rapidly rising rate of suicide. First, the increase in suicide closely parallels the increase in the divorce rate during the past 20 years (National Academy of Sciences, 1976; Nicholi, 1985). Second, the dramatic increase in the suicide rate among prepubescent children during the past 20 years indicates that many determinants of teenage suicide occur before adolescence. In addition, cohort analysis shows that each five-year cohort entering adolescence has a higher rate of suicide than the preceding five-year cohort, further suggesting that early childhood experiences play an important role in the increase in suicide (Murphy, Wetzel, 1980; Deykin, 1986). These data have prompted researchers to scrutinize the changes during the past few decades in child-rearing practices in the United States and in the homes of young children.

Divorce and out-of-wedlock pregnancies contribute to over half the children in the United States growing up in homes with one or both parents missing. Recent research demonstrates that among children and adolescents who commit suicide, a statistically significant number come from fragmented homes with missing parents. The fragmented home often consists of a missing father and a working mother with young children. Cantor (1972) found that 50 percent of adolescents who attempted suicide came from broken homes with the father absent; Tishler et al. (1981) found that in a sample of 108 adolescents who attempted suicide, 49 percent came from homes with one parent missing; other studies have found that the early loss or absence of a father played a significant role in adolescents who killed themselves (Paffenbarger, Asnes, 1966; McAnarney, 1979; Petzel, Riddle, 1981; Peck, 1982); other studies have found a statistically significant incidence of separation and divorce among adolescents who attempt suicide as compared with control groups (Marks, Heller, 1977; Goldney, 1982; Adams, Bouchoms, and Steiner, 1982; Deykin, 1986). What causes boys to commit suicide more than girls? Research again points to early childhood experiences and changes in the home. Most single-parent homes have absent fathers, and studies show that sons of absent fathers develop difficulty in controlling impulses. Male suicidal behavior results from an inability to control angry impulses (Trunnel, 1968; Tennant et al., 1981). Other studies show that both among nursery-school children and among adolescents, sons suffer more adverse effects than daughters when both parents work (Gold, Andres, 1978; McCord, McCord and Thurber, 1963; Propper, 1972).

During the past four decades a vast body of research has stressed the importance to the developing child of the physical presence and emotional accessibility of both parents. This research has demonstrated clearly that the absence of a parent through death, divorce, illness or a time-demanding job, contributes to many forms of emotional disorder, especially the anger, the low self-esteem, and the depression that accompany adolescent suicide. As the landmark report on families by the National Academy of Sciences (1976) succinctly states, the children at risk are children from homes in which one or both parents are frequently absent. The report notes that "in addition to needing food, shelter and basic health care, every child under six requires the constant care of an adult ... for millions of America's children, such care becomes problematic because ... both parents work." An overwhelming body of research indicates that any understanding of the epidemic of adolescent suicide must consider the role of physically and emotionally absent parents in the homes of American children and adolescents.

In summary, children experience an absent parent as rejection, and rejection inevitably breeds resentment and hostility. The child may express this outwardly in the form of violence or inwardly in the form of self-injury. These trends have resulted in our societies producing a staggering number of angry, depressed, and suicidal children. Research indicates clearly that a broken home with the resultant loss or absence of a parent predisposes a child to a variety of emotional disorders that manifest themselves immediately or later in the child's life.

Recommendations

We must as a nation begin to reshape our concept of the family, so that:

a) The family is given the highest priority in the functioning of all of our institutions from the federal government to the corner grocery store. The working hours of our institutions must be geared to husbands and wives spending part of every 24 hours with one

another and with their children. (The current
disorganized functioning of our Congress that keeps its
members from any sustained contact with their families
for days and sometimes weeks is a national disgrace
and an abhorrent model for the rest of the country.)

b) Schools and colleges inculcate the research findings
alluded to in this paper and other research that
indicates that fulfillment and happiness are closely
related to family relationships and love within those
relationships, that striving for individual status
ultimately proves empty and frustrating if gained at the
sacrifice of these relationships, that parents must be
free to stay home with young children if they have the
desire and the opportunity to do so, that time spent to
earn money for a second TV set, a second car, or even a
private school can never compensate for time with the
child as far as that child's well-being and quality of life
are concerned.

c) Our institutions make it possible for parents to work at
home as often as possible, abolishing outdated laws that
discourage this work. Conferences and conventions stop
taking spouses away from the family for days or weeks,
but include their families. Employers permit individuals
to refuse to be moved to another location so as not to
uproot the family, without fearing a demotion. Young
mothers who must work are provided facilities for
superb care of their children and time to visit them
during the day and flexible hours so as to be home when
their children return from school.

d) Divorce will be considered only as a last resort, after
every effort is made to resolve the conflicts in the
relationship. The myth of divorce — that portrays
divorce as merely a change of partners, like a new car or
new job — will be totally exposed. Courts of conciliation
will be established where lawyers will encourage — in
place of the adversary posture — a process of reconciliation, forgiveness, and a new beginning — if for no

other reason than for the emotional health of the
children.

*—Armand M. Nicholi, Jr., M.D., is associate clinical professor of
psychiatry at Harvard Medical School.*

REFERENCES

Adams, K.S., Bouchoms, A., and Steiner, D. 1982. Parental loss and family stability
in attempted suicide. *Archives of General Psychiatry* 39: 1081-85.
Baldwin, W. 1982. Trends in adolescent contraception, pregnancy, and child
rearing. In *Premature Adolescent Pregnancy and Parenthood*, ed. E.R. McAnarney. New York: Grune J. Stratton.
Bender, L. and Yarnell, H. 1941. An Observation Nursery: A Study of 250 Children
in the Psychiatric Division of Bellevue Hospital. *American Journal of Psychiatry*
97:1158-72.
Bowlby, J. 1940. The Influence of Early Environment in the Development of
Neurosis and Neurotic Character. *International Journal of Psycho-Analysis*
21:154-78.
—————————. 1951. *Maternal Care and Mental Health*. Geneva: WHO; London:
HMSD; New York: Columbia University Press. Abridged version (1965), *Child Care
and the Growth of Love*. 2nd ed. Harmondsworth, Middlesex: Penguin.
Bronfenbrenner, U. 1974. The Origins of Alienation. *Scientific American*. August,
pp. 53-61.
Burlingham, D.T. and Freud, A. 1942. *Young Children in War-Time: A Year's Work
in a Residential War Nursery*. London: Allen & Unwin.
—————————. 1943. *Infants Without Nurseries*. London: Allen & Unwin.
Cantor, P. 1972. The Adolescent Attempter. *Suicide and Life Threatening Behavior*
2:252-61.
Davis, P.A. 1983. *Suicidal Adolescents*. Springfield, Illinois: Thomas.
Deutsch, H. 1967. *Selected Problems of Adolescence*. New York: International Uni-
versities Press.
Deykin, E. 1986. Adolescent Suicide and Self-Destructive Behavior: An Interven-
tion Study. In *Suicide and Depression Among Adolescents and Young Adults*, ed.
G.L. Klerman. Washington, D.C.: American Psychiatric Press.
Frederick, C.H. 1985. An Introduction and Overview to Youth Suicide. In *Youth
Suicide*, ed. M.L. Peck, H.L. Faberow, and R.E. Litman. New York: Springer.
Glick, Paul. 1988. Remarried Families, Stepfamilies, and Stepchildren: A Brief
Demographic Profile. *Family Relations* 38:24-27.
Gold, D. and Andres, D. 1978. Relations Between Maternal Employment and
Development of Nursery School Children. *Canadian Journal of Behavioral Sci-
ence* 10:116-29.
Goldney, R.D. 1982. Locus of Control in Young Women Who Have Attempted
Suicide. *Journal of Nervous and Mental Disorders* 170:198.
Goldfarb, W. 1943. Infant Rearing and Problem Behavior. *American Journal of*

——————. 1951. Observations of Attitudes and Behavior in the Child Health Center. *American Journal of Public Health* 41: 182-190.

Levy, S.B. and Grinker, W.N. 1983. Choices and Life Circumstances — An Ethnographic Study of Project Redirection Teens. New York: Manpower Demonstration Research Corp.

Marks, P.A. and Heller, D.L. 1977. Now I Lay Me Down for Keeps: A Study of Adolescent Suicide Attempts. *Journal of Clinical Psychology* 33:340-400.

McAnarney, E.R. 1979. Adolescent and Young Adult Suicides in the United States: A Reflection of Societal Unrest. *Adolescence* 114:765-74.

McCord, J., McCord, W., and Thurber, E. The Effects of Maternal Employment on Lower Class Boys. *Journal of Abnormal Social Psychology* 67:167-82.

Murphy, G.E. and Wetzel, R.D. 1980. Suicide Risk by Birth Cohort in the U.S. *Archives of General Psychiatry* 37:519-25.

National Academy of Sciences. 1976. *Toward a National Policy for Children and Families*. Washington, D.C.

Nicholi, A.M., Jr. 1967. Harvard Dropouts: Some Psychiatric Findings. *American Journal of Psychiatry* 124:651-58.

——————. 1980. *Children and the Family*. Report of the Massachusetts Governor's Advisory Committee.

——————. 1983. The Non-Therapeutic Use of Psycho-Active Drugs: A Modern Epidemic. *New England Journal of Medicine* 308:925-33.

——————. 1985. The Impact of Parental Absence on Childhood Development: An Overview of the Literature. *Journal of Family and Culture* 1:19-28.

Nicholi, A.M., Jr., and Watt, N.F. 1976. Death of a Parent in the Etiology of Schizophrenia. In *Scientific Proceedings of the 129th Annual Meeting of the American Psychiatric Association*. Washington, D.C., 116-117.

Paffenbarger, R.S. and Asnes, D.P. 1966. Chronic Disease in Former College Students. III. Precursors of Suicide in Early and Middle Life. *American Journal of Public Health* 56:1026-36.

Peck, M.L. 1981. Teenage Suicide — A Tragic Impulse. *M.D.* February, pp. 49-52.

Petzel, S.V. and Riddle, M. 1981. Adolescent Suicide: Psychosocial and Cognitive Aspects. *Adolescent Psychiatry* 9:343-398.

Propper, A.M. 1972. The Relationship of Maternal Employment to Adolescent Roles, Activities and Parental Relationships. *Journal of Marriage and the Family* 34:417-21.

Rekers, G.A. 1983. Father Absence in the Broken Family: The Effects on Children's Development. *Oversight on the Breakdown of the Traditional Family Unit*. Washington, D.C.: U.S. Government Printing Office, 131-75.

Rekers, G.A., Mead, S.L., Rosen, A.C., and Brigham, S.L. 1983. Family Correlates of Male Childhood Gender Disturbance. *Journal of Genetic Psychology* 142:31-42.

Robertson, J. and Bowlby, J. 1952. Responses of Young Children to Separation from Their Mothers. *Courr. Cent. Int. Enf.* 2:131-42.

Rosenkrantz, A.L. 1978. A Note on Adolescent Suicide: Incidence, Dynamics and Some Suggestions for Treatment. *Adolescence* 13:209-14.

Shafii, M.S., Carrigan, S., Whittinghill, J. and Derrick, A. 1985. Psychological Autopsy of Completed Suicide in Children and Adolescents. *American Journal of Psychiatry* 142:1061-64.

Small, G.S. and Nicholi, A.M., Jr. 1982. Mass Hysteria Among School Children: Early Loss as a Predisposing Factor. *Archives of General Psychiatry* 39:721-24.

Spitz, R.A. 1946. Anaclytic Depression. *Psychoanalytic Study of Children* 2:313-42.

Tennant, C., Smith, A., Bubblington, P. and Harry J. 1981. Parental Loss in Childhood: Relationship to Adult Psychiatric Impairment and Contact with Psychiatric Services. *Archives of General Psychiatry* 38:309-14.

Tishler, C.L., McHenry, P.C. and Morgan, K.C. 1981. Adolescent Suicide Attempts: Some Significant Factors. *Suicide and Life Threatening Behavior* 11:86-92.

Trunnell, T.L. 1968. The Absent Father's Children's Emotional Disturbances. *Archives of General Psychiatry* 19:180-88.

U.S. Bureau of the Census. 1975. *Historical Statistics of the United States, Colonial Times to 1970*. Bicentennial Ed. Part 1. Washington, D.C.

——————. 1989. *Statistical Abstract of the United States: 1989*. 109th ed. Washington, D.C.

Wallerstein, J. 1980. The Impact of Divorce on Children. *Psychiatric Clinicians of North America*. 3:455-68.

Wallerstein, J. 1989. Children After Divorce: Wounds That Don't Heal. *The Psychiatric Times*. August, pp. 8-11.

Zwerling, I. 1978. Struggle for Survival. In *The American Family* (Unit 1, Report #4). Smith, Kline and French Laboratories, 5.

Family Structure and Crime

by Travis Hirschi

*Any influence within or without the family . . . which aids
the growing youngster to manage his primitive inclinations
. . . is a preventive of delinquency.* Per Contra, *the more the
instructive, protective, and supportive social institutions . . .
disintegrate and thereby lose their power to socialize . . . ,
the more will the natural impulses toward selfish, asocial
. . . or antisocial expression tend to flow into action* (Sheldon
Glueck, 1959: 126).

I t seems reasonable to begin a discussion of family structure and
crime with the assumption that the substantial increase in
single-parent families in recent years is somehow connected to the
high rate of crime and drug abuse in American society. Following
the logic of our epigraph, we could go further and suggest that the
connection is causal, that any loss of the instructive, protective, or
supportive power of the family will eventually show itself in higher
rates of deviant behavior. Having said this, we would then have to
recognize that the crime rate peaked about ten years ago, moved
down for about 5 years, and is only now approaching 1980 levels.
We would also have to recognize that drug use stabilized in the first
few years of the decade and has actually fallen since 1985. Yet
during this decade of stability and even decline in crime and drug
use, the two-parent family has continued to take a beating in the
statistics.

We are thus warned at the outset that the connection between
family structure and crime is probably not as strong as we are
sometimes inclined to assume. This warning is reinforced by the
conclusion of most research in the area: structural factors may well
be causally connected to crime, but their effects are small, and the
mediating or family functioning variables are so much stronger
that it is easy to account for the effects of the structural variables
and to find conditions in which they appear to have no effect at all.

Put another way, if we take the direct approach to the question
of the connection between family structure and crime, it is virtually

assured that we will come eventually to an unsatisfying conclusion. Others have stated it well: ". . . we should expect to find statistical associations with criminality that are partial, easily obscured by other factors, and heavily dependent on the nature of the sample and the measures of criminality" (Wilson and Herrnstein, 1985:248; see also Gove and Crutchfield, 1982:316).

Given this fact, it seems to me we would be well advised to approach the connection between family structure and crime only after we have satisfied ourselves that we know what to expect to find when we get there — only after we have constructed a theory and spelled out its implications for the role of the family in crime causation. Following this indirect approach, we can at least hope to get beyond the traditional conclusion that all is complex and difficult to a positive conclusion potentially useful to theory and policy.

The indirect approach takes us first to what we wish to explain, in this case crime. Michael Gottfredson and I have just published a book (Gottfredson and Hirschi, 1990) that concludes that ineffective child rearing is one of the major causes of crime. In writing this book, we found ourselves returning again and again to four facts. In our view, all argue one way or another for the importance of child rearing, and all are consistent with a particular conception of crime and its causes. Before introducing these facts, let me summarize the conceptual scheme from which we believe they can be derived.

Crime. We begin with the notion, not original to us, that all human acts are attempts to maximize pleasure and minimize pain. From this it follows that crimes are also attempts to increase pleasure and reduce pain. Crimes are distinguished from noncrimes by the fact that they are punished by the state. The state adds painful consequences to some acts in an effort to reduce the frequency of their occurrence. Generally, these are acts whose benefits clearly exceed their costs, at least in the short run, but which have directly painful consequences for others. Put another way, the state is generally interested in reducing the use of force and fraud for private or personal ends.

Once attention is called to the common elements in crimes, it is apparent that many noncriminal acts are analogous to them, that many acts not punished by the state also produce immediate gratification at the risk of long-term pain. Obvious examples are use of alcohol, tobacco, or drugs, truancy from school and work, promiscuous sex, overeating, and rock climbing.[1]

If we turn our attention to the behavior of children, it is not hard to see much of their pushing, shoving, hitting, screaming, and stealing as also analogous to crime — i.e., as displaying interest in immediate benefit without concern for the rights of others or for long–range costs.

Crimes, then, take little planning, skill, or effort. They and their analogs are available to everyone without training or tutelage. Given that they are governed by the desires of the moment and are in addition subject to long-term penalties, they may be expected to interfere with the attainment of ends requiring planning, skill, or effort.

Criminals. We assume that the nature of people relatively likely to engage in crimes can be derived from the nature of the acts themselves. Thus, offenders should be oriented to the pleasures of the moment and little concerned about long-term consequences. They should tend to lack diligence, tenacity, or persistence in a course of action. They should tend to pursue immediate pleasures that are not criminal; they should be more likely to party, to smoke, drink, gamble, and get pregnant before they are married.

We believe the evidence is substantially consistent with these inferences, that a stable, general trait or tendency underlies a broad range of criminal and noncriminal acts. We call this tendency low self-control. Let me summarize this evidence.

Versatility. Much evidence confirms that those committing any given criminal act are likely to commit other criminal acts as well, that tendencies among offenders to specialize in particular crimes are, to put it mildly, weak. As a result, it is misleading to speak of thieves, robbers, rapists, or burglars. In official data, the offender's prior and subsequent offenses are as likely as not to differ from the instant offense, with no apparent trend in sequences of offenses toward greater seriousness, sophistication, or specialization (e.g., Wolfgang, Figlio, and Sellin, 1972). Self-report data involving large numbers of delinquent and criminal acts routinely show that responses to all items are positively correlated (Hindelang, Hirschi, and Weis, 1981).

The versatility of offenders extends to noncriminal acts analogous to crime. Offenders are more likely to smoke, drink, use drugs

(Akers, 1984), skip school, and be involved in accidents. In many cases, the correlations between these offenses and criminal acts are as strong as those among criminal acts themselves, suggesting that the distinction between crimes and these particular noncriminal acts is artificial.

Versatility suggests that heinous crimes, trivial peccadillos, and indeed the ordinary self-indulgences of everyday life have the same functions for the individual or are produced by the same causes. Apparently, one feature criminal and deviant acts share is that they are ends in themselves, governed by proximate, direct, and transparent motives.

Immediacy. Most theories assume that the purposes or motives behind crimes are larger than those obvious in the acts themselves, that, for example, the motive behind theft is not goods or money, but success, self-esteem, or the good opinion of others; that the motive behind rape is not sex, but power, control, or hatred of women. Ironically, the search for large or general purposes behind crime leads to the expectation that offenders will favor some offenses to the exclusion of others, that they will tend to become more sophisticated, skillful, or careful over time. In fact, as we have seen, none of these tendencies can be detected in "criminal careers." We are led, then, to the conclusion that criminal and delinquent acts go together because each and all represent one of the myriad ways we can attempt to feel better or hurt less here and now.

If the impulse to a particular criminal or deviant act is fleeting and easily overcome by inconvenience or delay, the general tendency to engage in such acts appears to be made of more resistant material.

Stability. In fact, differences among people in the likelihood that they will commit criminal or analogous acts tend to persist over long periods of time, from childhood to adulthood. Psychologists studying aggression (Olweus, 1979), criminologists following children into their teens and "delinquents" into adulthood (Glueck and Glueck, 1968; West and Farrington, 1977; Shannon, 1981), all report that those high on crime or its analogs at early periods are likely to remain more likely to commit such acts after many years have passed (see also Robins, 1966).

Age and crime. Most criminologists agree that crime generally peaks in late adolescence or early adulthood and then declines rapidly to the end of life. A few years ago, we advanced the idea that this relation is in fact invariant over social and cultural conditions, that age has a direct, or, for all intents and purposes, an unmediated effect on crime. We believe the evidence also points to similar declines in offenses analogous to crime, in accidents, substance abuse, and illicit sexual activity.

So, we have a trait that is general (has implications for a broad range of behavior) and stable (differences between people are resistant to change), but declines sharply with age. Our trait is also weak in that it allows, but does not seem to require, deviant behavior. Those high on the tendency to commit criminal and analogous acts quickly lose interest in them as they are made more difficult, time consuming, or painful.

Self-Control. We believe the concept of self-control captures the relatively stable tendency to engage in (and avoid) a wide range of criminal, deviant, or reckless acts better than such traditional concepts as criminality, aggression, or conscience. Criminality suggests a specific propensity to crime contrary to the finding that "criminals" can get along quite well without crimes. It also suggests a tendency to specialize in criminal acts, a suggestion contrary to the finding that offenders are as likely to engage in the pursuit of noncriminal as criminal pleasures. Aggression has similar problems. In addition, it is not easily squared with the fact that the bulk of deviant acts are passive, surreptitious, or retreatist (e.g., theft and drug use). With its emphasis on restraint, conscience is closer than criminality to self-control. However, it too is more easily applied to sinful, immoral, or illegal acts than to imprudent acts; it has unfortunate connotations of compulsion, and it has not been much developed, even by those inclined to favor it.

The Family and the Facts. What do these facts say about the role of the family or child rearing in crime causation? The fact most obviously relevant to the family is the stability of differences in the likelihood of criminal and deviant behavior over the life course. These stable differences appear to be established as early as ages six to eight. They must therefore be traceable to training in the family, to inherited predispositions, or to some combination of training and predisposition. If the early "onset" of delinquency does not rule out biological inheritance, it devastates theories that ignore the family and assume teenage "desocialization" as a result of exposure to delinquent peer groups or to the American dream of monetary success.

The versatility finding is also significant for the institutional location of explanations of crime. If pushing, shoving, whining, and taking at an early age are equivalent to delinquency in adolescence and crime in adulthood, the family's stake in crime control is obvious, and many of the puzzles of crime research appear in a new light. Crime can be studied well before its "onset," and children can be trained to avoid criminal acts they are at the time incapable of committing.

Immediacy would seem to be the characteristic of criminal acts whose implications for child rearing is most in need of analysis. Under modern conditions of affluence and abundance, the possibilities for immediate satisfaction of transient wants are enormous, and it is often not obvious why these wants should be denied. Put another way, prosperity may reduce the value of self-control as it undermines the family's ability to produce it. We will try to return to this issue again in the context of research results.

The age finding indicates that by the time the family is normally done with the child (by the time it is no longer legally responsible), the crime years are rapidly coming to a close anyway. Put another way, if the family is able to keep the child out of trouble during the period it is responsible, the chances of later difficulty are small. Once again, the family does the job of crime control or it is not done at all.

We assume that people can be ranked on a continuum from high to low self-control. At the high end, child-rearing institutions and the exigencies of life have somehow built into some people generalized resistance or indifference to the pleasures of the moment. In exchange for their asceticism, these people disproportionately avoid the long-term physical, legal, and social costs such pleasures normally entail. At the low end of the self-control continuum, child-rearing institutions and the exigencies of life have somehow failed to build into other people the resistance described. In exchange for pleasures of the moment, these people bear disproportionately the long-term social, economic, and physical costs such pleasures normally entail.

Our analysis of the costs and benefits of self-control suggests that familial institutions, indeed all social institutions, will favor self-control over its absence. We are thus justified in the assumption that low self-control represents the failure of institutions to realize their values, that low self-control is evidence that something has gone wrong. We are now perhaps in position to face directly the role of the family in crime prevention. How might the family realize its interest in crime control?

1. *The family may reduce the likelihood of criminal behavior by socializing its children, by teaching them self-control.* If this much is given by previous analysis, the difficult question is how socialization is accomplished or self-control produced. In our view, the best "model" of this process is a statement of the conditions individually necessary and collectively sufficient for socialization to occur. I have previously described this model, derived from the parent-training program of the Oregon Social Learning Center (Patterson, 1980) and the research of Sheldon and Eleanor Glueck (1950), as containing four elements: caring for the child, monitoring the child's behavior, recognizing deviant behavior when it occurs, and punishing it (Hirschi, 1983). Such elementary training should condition the child to consider the long-range consequences of a wide variety of immediately pleasurable acts.

In the context of the present discussion and adjusting for criticism of the earliest model, I should more explicitly note that "caring" need not involve parental love, only an adult with sufficient stake in the socialization of the child to do what is necessary to produce it. "Recognizing deviant behavior" should now be replaced with "recognizing evidence of low self-control." While the former term implicitly recognizes that something equivalent to and more general than crime is required to describe the relevant behavior of children, it does not go far enough in recognizing the relevance of many forms of short-sighted behavior that are not necessarily deviant. Finally, something like "correct" should be substituted for "punish." The latter term was justified earlier to highlight the inappropriateness of emphasizing rewards over penalties, but its unsavory connotations remain so strong in the minds of many that it should probably be replaced by a milder term.

Patterson's original parent-training model (1980) was much more complex than the model I extracted from it. He now reports no success in attempts to show the importance of such "fine tuning variables" as parent involvement, positive reinforcement, and problem solving: "Although we have put a great deal of time and effort into building these constructs, they do not seem to account for any of the variance in predicting achievement or antisocial behavior other than what we already have in our measures of monitoring and discipline" (Patterson, 1989).

In a recent reanalysis of the Gluecks' data, Laub and Sampson (1988) show the primacy of the parent-child variables described by the model (and their ability to account for the family structure variables found to be important by the Gluecks). A recent meta-analysis of the research literature on the family and delinquency (Loeber and Stouthamer-Loeber, 1986) reaches similar conclusions. (In all candor, I must say however that it is often hard to know what meaning to attach to the whole body of research in the family-delinquency area. This research tradition has been guided by such diverse concepts, many inadequately defined or measured, that its bearing on some elements of the minimal model of child rearing, especially "recognition" and "discipline," is problematic.)

I continue to believe that a simple model is all the research literature can sustain. For example, when Wilson and Herrnstein summarize the results of research as showing separate etiologies for aggressive children and thieves, they inadvertently run into serious trouble with the facts: "The irritable parent who does not use discipline effectively tends to produce aggressive children; the indifferent and ineffective parent tends to produce larcenous ones. In the first case, the child discovers he can bully his parents; in the second, that he can evade them" (1985:230). Unfortunately for conclusions about the differential effects of child-rearing practices, there is no good evidence for the existence of the distinct types allegedly produced by them. As we have seen, aggression and larceny (and drug abuse and truancy) tend to come wrapped together in the same package.

In fact, one way to test our model is to examine its general application to a wide range of acts. Alternative models often suggest specific consequences for specific patterns of child–rearing or complex interactions among family conditions and child–rearing practices. Our model suggests, again, that such analyses mistake differences in the form of delinquent acts for differences in their causal content. If we are correct, the child–rearing correlates of theft, aggressiveness, drug use, future orientation, achievement orientation, completion of homework, and grade point average (to take only a sample of indicators of self-control) should be, for all intents and purposes, the same.

Table 1 displays the correlations between parental supervision in the Richmond data (Hirschi, 1969) and measures of the variables listed above. In all cases, the correlations are (1) in the predicted direction, and (2) roughly comparable in magnitude, findings consistent with the idea that crime is a species of low self-control, a general trait produced by parental socialization practices.

Let us then move on to another aspect of family child-rearing practice.

2. *The family may reduce the likelihood of delinquency by restricting its children's activity, by maintaining actual physical surveillance of them, and by knowledge of their whereabouts when they are out of sight.* Parental supervision should be an important variable in its own right, as well as a component variable in a socialization model. Supervision gains its prominence in our scheme through the general youthfulness of offenders and the immediacy of the rewards produced by their delinquent acts. In my first look at this question, I concluded that direct parental control was of little "substantive or theoretical importance" (Hirschi, 1969:88). This conclusion stemmed from awareness of the brevity of delinquent acts (a property closely related to the immediacy of their benefits) and of the freedom enjoyed by most adolescents. But if brevity makes surveillance more difficult, immediacy makes it more profitable. The would-be offender can often do what he wants to do in a hurry, but if he is unable to do so, he is unlikely to persist in the effort. By the same token, adolescents may be relatively free today compared to adolescents in the past, but they remain relatively restricted compared to adults, and there is enough variation among families in this regard to make a difference, at least potentially.

3. *The family may reduce the likelihood of delinquency by commanding the love, respect, or dependence of its members.* A self- or social-control explanation of crime may focus on the enduring effects of socialization or on the current effects of ties to controlling institutions. In point of fact, the two effects are difficult to separate because those high on self-control are likely to be well integrated into such institutions. For example, the student high on self-control will do his homework, do well in school, and consequently like

Table 1. Correlations between parental supervision [Four items: Does your mother (father) know where you are (whom you are with) when you are away from home?], mother's supervision (two items), number of siblings, and various indicators of self control.

| | Supervision | | Number of |
	Parental*	Mother's**	Siblings***
Smoking and drinking	-.30	-.27	.12
Self-reported violence	-.25	-.23	.10
Self-reported theft	-.29	-.27	.12
Offenses on police records	-.10	-.14	.15
Finish homework	.22	.20	-.11
Future orientation	.13	.13	-.12
Achievement orientation	.17	.18	.01 (n.s.)
Grade point average—English	.17	.16	-.17

All correlations significant at .001 level. *N's range from 1004 to 1187. **N=822. ***N's range from 1123 to 1547.

school. When attachment to the school predicts nondelinquency, as it does, we cannot know without further self-analysis whether it does so because of self- or social-control.

The same is true for attachment to or respect for parents. These attachments presumably produce conformity in their own right and also make socialization easier. (It is easier for the parent to correct a child who values the parent's opinion.) Our theory suggests that, for persons attached to controlling institutions, conformity carries its own rewards, and its explicit acknowledgment is therefore unnecessary. An alternative model stresses the idea that the power parents command as a result of the child's attachment is reduced if it is not exercised (Wilson and Herrnstein, 1985:235). The issue is then whether the child's attitude toward the parents is important irrespective of its connection to their ability to reinforce the child's behavior.

4. *The family may reduce crime by guarding the home, by protecting it from potential thieves, vandals, and burglars.* Criminological theory traditionally focused on offenders rather than on offenses and assumed that offenders were powerfully motivated to commit their crimes, especially "serious" crimes. Once the focus shifted to criminal events it became evident that offenders were not all that skillful, all that motivated, or all that dangerous. In fact, it soon became plain that familial institutions may play a role in crime control beyond watching their own members, that they can do much by merely protecting their own property. Further, it became clear that to do so effectively they need not brandish weapons or cower behind locked doors. The mere presence of a family member in the house or on the property is enough to deter the typical offender interested in burglary or theft. As a result, a major predictor of the burglary rate in an area is the proportion of homes occupied during the day, a proportion clearly affected by family structure (Cohen and Felson, 1979).

5. *The family may reduce delinquency by protecting its members, by deterring potential fornicators, assaulters, molesters, and rapists.* Deterring potential burglars is one thing, deterring those interested in sex with or revenge on family members is another. Lone women and women-only families are at unusual risk from male predators, both inside and outside the home. (And children in families with stepparents, especially stepfathers, also run unusual risks of sexual and physical abuse.) The situation described by

Judith Blake in Jamaica must exist at least in attenuated form in many households whose defense can enlist no adult males:

> One of the most important and effective ways of protecting young girls from sexual exploitation is for male relatives to be ready and able to retaliate if such exploitation occurs. Whether this condition prevails depends heavily on the organization of the family. . . . Among lower-class Jamaicans, however, a father is as likely as not to be absent from the family picture. Brothers may be merely half-brothers, or living elsewhere. . . . The sexual exploitation of young girls therefore both results from family disorganization and contributes to it. Men are provided with a far wider range of sexual partners than they would be if girls were protected. Thus, there are fewer pressures on the man to form a permanent liaison. Moreover, once a woman has a child or two, her desirability can always be weighted by men against that of the childless young girl. Thus, because young girls are in many ways unprotected from male advances, older women are unprotected from the competition of young girls (Blake, 1961:89, quoted by Hartley, 1975:67).

6. *Finally, the family may reduce delinquency by acting as an advocate for the child, as a probation or parole agency willing to guarantee the good conduct of its members.* At all levels of the criminal justice system, community or family ties are taken into account in processing decisions. The individual with no family to vouch for him is likely to penetrate the system further than the person whose family is willing to take responsibility for his conduct. It is sometimes said, in fact, that the criminal justice system tends to avoid intervention whenever it has an excuse for doing so. An extended, stable family obviously concerned for the offender's welfare makes a very good excuse indeed.

Now we are ready to turn to family structure and its implications for crime. Let us go directly to what appears to be the major structural trend of modern time — the increasing prevalence of the mother-only family.

The single-parent or mother-only family. Our socialization model suggests that, all else equal, one parent may be enough. Earlier, I argued that "all else is rarely equal" (Hirschi, 1983:62), emphasizing the limits on the single parent's ability to monitor the child and punish deviant behavior. The present analysis suggests even further difficulties for the single parent. She is likely to be less able to restrict her children's activity, less able to protect them from predators, less able to guard the house in which they live, and less able to guarantee their good conduct to the school and the criminal justice system. All of this would make her appear less effective than the two-parent family, even if it said little or nothing about the actual behavior of her children.

Clearly, we are again in danger of building an argument contrary to observed differences that can rarely be characterized as large. Before proceeding further, we should examine the differences between single-parent and double-parent families on measures of delinquency available to us and compare these differences with those produced by comparable research (table 2).

To my mind, the similarities in table 2 between the results of the Richmond Youth Study (Hirschi, 1969) and those reported by Dornbusch et al. (1985) for the National Health Examination Survey are remarkable, given the fact that the first is a local and the second a national sample. Both tend to show differences of the same magnitude between the single-parent and double-parent family. These differences are in the expected direction. They are, however, small, at least compared to those observed for the family functioning variables such as supervision, and are, in some cases, too small to reach significance, even with the large samples involved.

The data in table 2 would seem to confirm the view that family structure is especially important for forms of deviance that involve the reaction of other institutions (the police and the school). Thus, in the Richmond data, the self-report delinquency scale, made up of theft, fighting, and vandalism items, is unrelated to the parental makeup of the home, as is a combination measure of smoking and drinking. At the same time, the official measure of delinquency and items measuring difficulty with the school show differences favoring the two-parent family. All of which suggests that the effects on crime of the parental makeup of the family may be explained through examination of its role as advocate for the child. Apparently, the mother alone is especially handicapped in dealing with other institutions responsible for the child's conduct (Fenwick, 1982).

Dornbusch et al. (1985) report that youth in mother-only households are slightly more likely than youth in two-parent

Table 2. Percent of adolescents deviant by parental makeup of home. Dornbusch *et al.*, 1985, and Richmond Youth Project data (Hirschi, 1969).

	Two Natural Parents		Natural Mother		
% police record (Richmond—white males)	23.4	(1113)	30.5 (226)		(.01)
% law contact (Dornbusch—all males)	26.0	(2744)	36.0 (382)		(.01)
% truant — self-report (Richmond—white males)	14.9	(1078)	19.7 (218)		(.01)
% truant — school records (Dornbusch—all males)	1.0	(2501)	6.0 (318)		(.001)
% reporting delinquent acts (Richmond, white males)	60.7	(1083)	61.2 (219)		(n.s.)
% suspended—self report (Richmond—white males)	19.6	(1080)	27.2 (217)		(.05)
% school discipline (Dornbusch—all males)	35.0	(2303)	47.0 (291)		(.001)
% smoke (Richmond — black males*)	29.4	(384)	34.5 (182)		(.10)
% smoke regularly (Dornbusch — all males)	15.0	(2760)	20	(385)	(.001)

Numbers are in parentheses. *White males not significant.

households to be allowed to make their own decisions, but that this difference does not account for the observed effect of family structure. The difference in decision-making power in the Richmond data is even smaller and given the smaller sample size does not reach statistical significance. Perhaps more significant is the finding that only about 1 in 10 white males reports being free to make his own decisions, whatever the parental makeup of the family. The figure for black males suggests even greater parental control, with about 1 in 15 (6.6. percent) saying that decisions are made by them rather than jointly with their mothers or by their mothers alone.

As expected, however, the child from the single-parent family is, according to his own reports, less well supervised than the child from the two–parent family — by both his mother and father. There is, then, at least in the eyes of the child, no tendency for the mother to compensate for the absence of her husband by increasing her own supervision. Whereas 59 percent of children in two-parent families report that their mothers always know where they are and whom they are with, the comparable figure for children in mother-only families is 51 percent. (For the father, these figures are 51 percent and 39 percent, indicating that mother's knowledge of the child's whereabouts under unfavorable conditions is still as good as father's under favorable conditions.)

A related fact seems worth mentioning. When asked what would be the worst thing about being caught for stealing, children from two-parent families are significantly more likely than children from mother-only families to mention the reaction of parents [52 percent vs. 41 percent (.001)] (see also Steinberg, 1987). If crime may be prevented by a moment's hesitation, a second parent in the child's active social network may make the difference between crime and noncrime.

The single-parent family is consistently shown to be economically disadvantaged compared to the double-parent family (Garfinkel and McLanahan, 1986:12-15), a fact that would at one time have been taken to have considerable significance for crime. Our analysis grants only a minor and uncertain role to the economic status of the family in crime causation. Such neglect is justified on several grounds: (1) Research of the kind available to me has for many years found little or no relation between family socioeconomic status and delinquency. (2) Our theoretical perspective sees crime as noneconomic activity, as leading to economic disaster rather than to economic success. (3) It explicitly denies that offenders are driven to crime by need, deprivation, or poverty. In fact, the theory is inclined in the other direction, tending to see poverty as teaching people to forego current pleasure in the hope of long-term reward (Durkheim, 1951). (In this connection, several studies report a positive relation between spending money and drug use in juvenile populations.)

Finally, the finding that membership in mother-only families has a negative effect on intelligence test scores (Garfinkel and McLanahan, 1986:28) is certainly relevant. In a range of studies, these scores have been shown to be negatively related to delinquency. In the Richmond data, the family structure, IQ test, delinquency correlations are consistent with previous research. Children from single-parent families score lower on the Differential Aptitude Verbal Test (r=.08 (.01)), and children scoring low on the test are more likely to be delinquent (r=-.20 (.001)). A major correlate of these test scores is orientation toward time, with low scorers being much more likely to be oriented to the present than to the future. This orientation is, itself, a species of delinquency (see table 1).

In sum, the single-parent family appears to have a small impact on crime through its effects on supervision and academic achievement. The child of the single parent is more likely to have a here-and-now orientation to life and seems slightly more likely to have trouble interacting with adults. The latter problem shows itself in measures of deviant behavior based on the reactions of adults to the behavior of the child, where the effects of family structure are more evident than for deviant acts reported by the child alone. All of these statements, it should be recalled, are based on small, if statistically significant, differences.

Size of Family. I once characterized "size of family" as "an empiricist's dream" (Hirschi, 1969:239). It is not hard to see why. Size of family is consistently positively related to delinquency and consistently resists statistical explanation. The third column of table 1 shows that size of family, operationalized as number of siblings, predicts a variety of indicators of self-control. Table 3 shows that the effects of number of siblings are stronger than the effects of the parental structure of the home when attention is restricted to those measures of deviant behavior previously shown to be affected by parental structure.

Table 3. Percent of adolescents deviant by number of siblings, white males, Richmond Youth Project.

	Number of Siblings						
	0	1	2	3	4	5+	r
% police record	14	22	23	28	31	43	.17
% truant	37	32	31	36	37	52	.09
% self-report del.	57	70	68	72	69	78	.11
% suspended	20	18	22	23	25	35	.11
% smoke	20	20	21	25	32	35	.12
Numbers	97–	380–	403–	269–	143–	178–	
	100	396	419	283	157	192	

Table 4. Percent with police record by parental makeup of home and number of siblings, white males, Richmond Youth Project.

	Parental Makeup of Home		
Number of Siblings	Two Natural Parents	Natural Mother Only	
0	12	18	
	(68)	(17)	(n.s.)
1	19	32	
	(300)	(47)	(.01)
2	21	21	
	(314)	(34)	(n.s.)
3	25	32	
	(197)	(44)	(n.s.)
4	31	19	
	(113)	(21)	(n.s.)
5 or more	36	38	
	(105)	(55)	(n.s.)
Totals*	23	30	
	(1113)	(226)	(.01)

*Totals are from table 2.

This finding leads to interest in the joint effects on delinquency of parental structure and number of siblings. These effects are shown in table 4, using police record as the measure of crime because it is predicted best by both structural factors.

A reasonable interpretation of table 4 might be that "number of siblings" more or less accounts for the effect on delinquency of the parental makeup of the home. In the Richmond data, single-parent families tend to be larger than two parent families (25 percent of the former as opposed to 10 percent of the latter have 6 or more children) and for that reason appear to be more conducive to delinquency.

As far as I can now determine, single-parent families are in fact often larger than intact or double-parent families — i.e., this phenomenon does not appear to be unique to the Richmond data (see Blake, 1985; Glueck and Glueck, 1950, p. 120). If so, the family size effect provides a potentially important alternative interpretation of the finding of differences in delinquency associated with the parental makeup of the home.

Given the magnitude of the family-size effect on delinquency, it deserves an attempt at systematic explanation. Let me, then, briefly assess the relevance of size to each of the devices available to the family for delinquency prevention.

Socialization / self-control. It is easy to find reasons to believe that large families may experience greater difficulties than small families in teaching self-control. The greater the number of children in the family, the greater the "dilution" of material and cultural resources (Blake, 1989, pp. 10-12). Parents with many children have less time, energy, and money to devote to each of them. Children in large families are likely to spend more time with other children and less time with adults, a situation not conducive to intellectual growth or general maturity.

Whatever one may think of these assertions, the fact is that children from large families score lower on intelligence tests (especially those tests that emphasize vocabulary or verbal ability), get poorer grades in school, expect to obtain less education, and actually complete fewer years of schooling than children from small families (Blake, 1989). The Richmond data confirm these findings.[2] They also confirm that all of these consequences of large family size are important correlates of delinquency.

We may thus conclude that an important reason large families are less effective than small families in controlling the delinquency potential of their children is that they are less effective in fostering verbal ability and academic success. Put in these terms, these findings seem to reflect the importance of the child-dominated intellectual atmosphere of the large family rather than its restricted material resources. In any event, because family size continues to affect delinquency when verbal ability, school grades, and educational expectations are controlled by statistical adjustment, this cannot be the whole story.[3]

Supervision. The idea that parents in large families have greater difficulty supervising their children seems to follow directly from the idea that such parents have less time and energy to devote to them. In fact, however, direct supervision is so much more efficient with large than with small numbers that it is not hard to imagine parents in large families doing more rather than less of it. Indirect supervision, keeping track of children who are out of sight, may well be a different matter, but here too the effects of size are not obvious.

In the Richmond study, children from very large families (6 or more children) are less likely to report that their parents always know where they are and whom they are with, and children from large families also report spending less time talking with their parents, but these differences are small and do not really begin to account for the effect of family size on delinquency. For that matter, there is reason to believe that even the small supervision differences may be partially misleading. As we have seen, children from very large families tend to score low on tests of verbal ability. Children with limited verbal ability are less likely to enjoy school. They are therefore more likely to truant and take up with the wrong crowd. As a result, they are more likely to report that on occasion their parents do not know where they are or whom they are with. The large family may thus cause "poor supervision" through its effect on verbal ability. Along the same lines, the standard supervision hypothesis does not really square with the fact that number of children living at home is *less* predictive of delinquency than the total number of children in the family.

Attachment to parents. Children from large families are slightly more likely to report having felt unwanted by their parents (r=.10 (.001)), but differences on such items as "Do you share your thoughts and feelings with your parents?" and "Would you like to be the kind of person your mother is?" do not reach statistical significance, even with the large sample available. Once again, then, although the data are consistent with the thrust of our explanatory scheme, they do not allow us to conclude that the family-size effect has been fully explained.[4]

As of now, then, it seems that in addition to its effects on deviant behavior through verbal ability, supervision, and attachment, number of children in the family has an effect on deviant behavior unexplained by the variables available to our analysis. We are thus free to speculate about other reasons for the relation between family size and crime. Because my interpretation of the family-size variable was initially greeted with such enthusiasm by participants in the conference held in Rockford, Illinois, I will repeat that discussion here. (The snippet of poetry, which perhaps says it all, is new.)

Recall that our self-control theory explicitly applies to all ages, to children, adolescents, and adults. It does not assume that adults are fully socialized or that children are universally unsocialized. On the contrary, it assumes that differences in self-control appear early and continue to manifest themselves throughout life. Recall, too, that the theory is inherently skeptical of the ability of institutions to affect behavior, especially when these institutions are organized and managed by people inclined to neglect the long-term interests of the institution whenever they conflict with their own short-term or immediate interests.

So, our theory suggests that size of family predicts deviant behavior in the children because it is itself an indicator of parental self-control. ('When my father got me, his mind was not on me' — A.E. Housman.) This suggestion does not seem particularly far-fetched when the children are born to unmarried women. After all, premarital pregnancy is probably as good a measure of delinquency among girls as we are likely to find. But if family size accounts for differences in delinquency between one-parent and two-parent families, it must affect delinquency within such families as well (see table 4). No one would suggest that bearing children within marriage is itself deviant behavior. However, behavior analogous to crime is clearly involved in the process, and we should perhaps therefore not be surprised to find that such behavior by parents predicts theoretically equivalent behavior in their children.

This hypothesis should be fairly easy to test. Size of family should have little or no effect when direct measures of parental self-control (e.g., criminal record) are taken into account. This hypothesis also has reasonably direct policy implications. It appears that we should worry less about strengthening the family to prevent crime and more about training people in self-control to strengthen the family.

Discussion. This paper began with the idea that family structure has a small and variable effect on crime, an effect that is easily accounted for by measures of family functioning or process. It ends on a rather different note, arguing that family size has a robust effect on delinquency that is not accounted for by its effects on supervision or attitudes toward parents. I should have known better than to fall for the idea that the consequences of such hard facts as number of parents and number of children depend on their meaning or interpretation. This idea may be resilient and plausible, but it is also a snare and a delusion. The number of parents and siblings does make a difference. In terms of deviant behavior, it is better to have two of one and few of the other.

This paper also began with the idea that the current trend in marital stability is unfavorable with respect to crime. It should end by noting a perhaps more important trend in family structure that is grounds for considerable optimism about the crime problem. According to Judith Blake (1989, p. 285), "Children in the United States are just beginning, on a large scale, to accrue some of the advantages of being brought up in small families. . . . [T]hese children should be the most fortunate and favored of any in our history. Even if . . . there is some deterioration in family stability and a corresponding rise in single parenthood, the decline in family size will offer compensation."

—Travis Hirschi is professor of public policy at the University of Arizona.

ENDNOTES

[1]Modern states are ambivalent about many of these acts. On the one hand, they are inclined to sanction them to prevent individuals from doing harm to themselves. On the other hand, they are inclined to do what they can to make their natural consequences less dangerous or painful. In this context, some advocates of drug

legalization argue that the least expensive and most consistent policy is to let nature take its course — i.e., let the health consequences of drugs control their use.

[2]In the sample of white males in grades 7-12 represented in tables 1-4, number of children is correlated -.16 with Differential Aptitude Test (DAT) verbal scores, -.09 with DAT space relations scores, -.16 with grade point average in English, and -.20 with educational expectations (based on 1,275 or more cases). These correlations are in most cases smaller among students in the 11th and 12th grades (and correspondingly larger among students in grades 7-10), a finding consistent with the idea that samples of college students are inadequate for assessing the effects of family size on academic ability. These correlations also maintain among Catholic, non-Catholic, single-parent, and two-parent families. In my view, these results cast further doubt on research and speculation to the effect that family size has different consequences among pro-family religious groups (see also Blake, 1989, p. 103).

[3]Such analysis shows that, of these variables, grade point average in English is the strongest predictor of delinquency. It shows, too, that educational expectations have no effect on delinquency when ability and performance are taken into account. In other words, educational expectations do not help explain the effect of family size on delinquency.

[4]In the interests of closure, it should be mentioned that the large family may be better able than the small family to guard the home and protect its members from predators. To the extent this is true, the reduction in crime from a trend toward small families would be smaller than previous analysis suggests. Finally, important differences between large and small families in the effectiveness of their intervention with the criminal justice system and the school are not apparent in the data. For example, large family size predicts smoking about as well as it predicts suspension from school.

REFERENCES

Blake, Judith. 1961. *Family Structure in Jamaica.* Glencoe, Illinois: Free Press.

———. 1985. "Number of Siblings and Educational Mobility." *American Sociological Review* 50:84-94.

———. 1989. *Family Size and Achievement.* Berkeley: University of California Press.

Cohen, Lawrence, and Marcus Felson. 1979. "Social Change and Crime Rate Trends: A Routine Activity Approach." *American Sociological Review* 44:588-608.

Dornbusch, Sanford, *et al.* 1985. "Single Parents, Extended Households, and the Control of Adolescents." *Child Development* 56:326-341.

Durkheim, Emile. 1951. *Suicide.* Glencoe, Illinois: Free Press.

Fenwick, Charles R. 1982. "Juvenile Court Intake Decision Making: The Importance of Family Affiliation." *Journal of Criminal Justice* 10:443-453.

Garfinkel, Irwin, and Sara S. McLanahan. 1986. *Single Mothers and Their Children: A New American Dilemma.* Washington, D.C.: The Urban Institute Press.

Glueck, Sheldon, ed. 1959. *The Problem of Delinquency.* Boston: Houghton Mifflin.

Glueck, Sheldon, and Eleanor Glueck. 1950. *Unraveling Juvenile Delinquency.* Cambridge, MA: Harvard University Press.

—————. 1968. *Delinquents and Nondelinquents in Perspective*. Cambridge: Harvard University Press.

Gottfredson, Michael, and Travis Hirschi. 1990. *A General Theory of Crime*. Stanford: Stanford University Press.

Gove, Walter and Robert Crutchfield. 1982. "The Family and Juvenile Delinquency." *The Sociological Quarterly* 23:301-19.

Hartley, Shirley Foster. 1975. *Illegitimacy*. Berkeley: University of California Press.

Hindelang, Michael, Travis Hirschi, and Joseph Weis. 1981. *Measuring Delinquency*. Beverly Hills: Sage.

Hirschi, Travis. 1983. "Crime and the Family." Pp. 53-68 in *Crime and Public Policy*, ed. J.Q. Wilson. San Francisco: Institute for Contemporary Studies Press.

—————. 1969. *Causes of Delinquency*. Berkeley: University of California Press.

Laub, John, and Robert Sampson. 1988. "Unraveling Families and Delinquency: A Reanalysis of the Gluecks' Data." *Criminology* 26:355-380.

Loeber, Rolf, and Magda Stouthamer-Loeber. 1986. "Family Factors as Correlates and Predictors of Juvenile Conduct Problems and Delinquency." Pp. 29-149 in *Crime and Justice: An Annual Review of Research*, Vol. 7. Ed. by M. Tonry and N. Morris. Chicago: University of Chicago Press.

Olweus, Dan. 1979. "Stability of Aggressive Reaction Patterns in Males: A Review." *Psychological Bulletin* 86:852-875.

Patterson, Gerald. 1980. "Children Who Steal." Pp. 73-90 in T. Hirschi and M. Gottfredson, *Understanding Crime*. Beverly Hills: Sage.

—————. 1989. Personal communication.

Robins, Lee. 1966. *Deviant Children Grown Up*. Baltimore: Williams & Wilkins.

Shannon, Lyle. 1981. Assessing the Relationship of Adult Criminal Careers to Juvenile Careers. Final Report. Washington, D.C.: NIJJDP.

Steinberg, Laurence. 1987. "Single Parents, Stepparents, and the Susceptibility of Adolescents to Antisocial Peer Pressure." *Child Development* 58:269-275.

West, Donald and David Farrington. 1977. *The Delinquent Way of Life*. London: Heinemann.

Wilson, James Q. and Richard Herrnstein. 1985. *Crime and Human Nature*. New York: Simon and Schuster.

Wolfgang, Marvin, Robert Figlio, and Thorsten Sellin. 1972. *Delinquency in a Birth Cohort*. Chicago: University of Chicago Press.

Family Dissolution and the Health Care Crisis

by Bryce J. Christensen

American policymakers in the late 20th century face few problems more daunting than that of runaway medical costs. Total national health expenditures rose from $74 billion in 1970 to $458 billion in 1986.[1] Real per capita spending on health care has climbed more than five times faster than productivity over the past two decades.[2] The rise in health-care costs paid by government has been even steeper, from $28 billion in 1970 to $190 billion in 1986. The expenses of a single government program — Medicare — have risen from just $7 billion in 1970 to $78 billion in 1986.[3] To date, policymakers have achieved only meager success in their efforts to contain costs through price controls, health maintenance organizations, and physician reviews. National health-care costs are projected to rise to $1.5 trillion by the year 2000 and to a staggering $2 trillion by the year 2030.[4]

As concern grows over the crisis in medical spending, some analysts now believe that the problem cannot be resolved without considering significant changes in American family life. Although only individual Americans can decide how to order their family lives, a growing body of research reveals that such decisions profoundly affect how much of the nation's wealth must be spent on medical care.

Evidence linking health and family life is not hard to find. Writing recently in *Social Science and Medicine*, Catherine K. Riessman and Naomi Gerstel observed that "one of the most consistent observations in health research is that married [people] enjoy better health than those of other marital statuses." Riessman and Gerstel noted that compared to married men and women, the divorced and separated suffer much higher rates of disease morbidity, disability, mental neuroses, and mortality. "This pattern has been found for every age group (20 years and over), for both men and women, and for both whites and nonwhites."[5]

In a paper presented in November 1988 to the American Public Health Association, Charlotte A. Schoenborn and Barbara F.

Wilson reported that the distinctive healthiness of married Americans has persisted despite recent changes in marriage and divorce rates. Examining data from a 1987 survey of 47,240 households comprising over 122,000 people, Schoenborn and Wilson discovered that, overall, "married persons had fewer health problems than unmarried persons." They observed that among those surveyed "married men were less likely to be limited in their activities than were single, divorced, or widowed men . . . a similar even stronger relationship was found for women." The health gap showed up especially among the middle-aged: among those 45 to 64 years old, one-third of single men and women suffered chronic disability compared with only one-fifth of the married. "In spite of the recent changes in American marital patterns," remark Schoenborn and Wilson, "there was still a clear association between being well and being married in 1987." The researchers further suggest that the "surge in divorces" in recent decades has imposed "hidden health costs on the American population" that should be recognized.[6]

Nor is there anything peculiar to this century or this country about the link between marriage and health. In a genealogical study of upper-class Europeans during the 16th, 17th, 18th, and 19th centuries, Sigismund Peller established that "mortality of married men always has been more favorable — especially in the ages below 50 — than that of bachelors." Although Peller found relatively high mortality rates among the married women during the 16th and 17th centuries (due in large part to deaths in childbirth), he found that mortality rates improved dramatically for married women over the centuries while mortality rates for unmarried women under age 50 improved more slowly.[7] William Farr noted a fairly consistent link between marriage and mortality in a study focused on mid-19th century France. Probably because of deaths in childbirth, Farr did find higher death rates among married women than among unmarried women aged 20 to 25. Among women aged 25 to 30, death rates were slightly lower among the married than among the unmarried. Among women over age 30 and among men over age 20, Farr documented a significantly lower mortality rate among the married than among the unmarried. "Marriage is a healthy estate," Farr concluded. "The single individual is more likely to be wrecked on his voyage than the lives joined together in matrimony."[8]

In a much more recent study published in 1987, demographers at Princeton University analyzed "a small group of developed countries representing a range of cultures (Sweden, Japan, England and Wales, and United States whites)" and found that "in all cases, despite any differences in marriage behavior that may exist, married persons experience lower mortality rates" than single, divorced, and widowed peers. The Princeton team then broadened their survey to 26 developed countries ranging from Austria to New Zealand to Singapore. Across all those cultures, the results were similar: "It is clear that in developed countries married persons of both sexes experience a marked mortality advantage relative to single individuals."[9]

Researchers are still trying to clarify the reasons for the linkage between marriage and good health. In a study published in 1962, Joseph Berkson admitted that "powers of explanation seem to fail" when trying to account for the fact that death rates run consistently higher for singles than for marrieds and higher for the divorced than for singles, not only overall, but for "such diverse disease groups as heart disease and cancer, arteriosclerosis and benign neoplasms, suicide and appendicitis, peptic ulcers and tuberculosis, nephritis, accidents, and bronchitis." Berkson thought it unlikely that "the more favorable environment of the married" could account for this mortality pattern for so many different types of diseases, some of which are actually aggravated by richer diets. Perhaps, Berkson conjectured, "differences of death rates may be determined constitutionally, rather than environmentally."[10]

Debra Umberson shed more light on the subject in a study published in 1987. She found that mortality rates ran consistently lower for parents than for adults who are not parents and for the married than for the unmarried, because marriage and parenthood both exert a "deterrent effect on health-compromising behaviors" such as excessive drinking, drug use, risk-taking, and disorderly living. By providing a system of "meaning, obligation, [and] constraint," family relationships markedly reduce the likelihood of unhealthy practices. Consonant with previous research, Umberson's study found that "although the effects of parenting status appear to be similar for men and for women . . . the unmarried state is more detrimental to men's health behaviors than to women's." Umberson's data further established that the health-protecting effects of family life are strongest for married couples with children still living at home and that the divorced practice poorer health habits than the widowed.[11]

Further evidence of the relationship between divorce and poor health habits comes from John Clausen of the University of California at Berkeley. Clausen's research leads him to believe that both divorce and smoking may be traced to a common personality profile. According to Clausen, young people with "planful competence" (people who are "thoughtful, self-confident and responsible") tend to avoid both divorce and smoking, while young people evincing little planful competence tend to become heavy smokers early in life and to divorce in subsequent years. High school students who score in "the bottom third of the index on 'planful competence' in the high school years were three to five times as likely to become divorced as those in the top third," with related statistics showing a "significant correlation between divorce and amount smoked for both men and women."[12]

Yet healthful habits alone cannot fully account for the health–enhancing effects of marriage. In a study at Ohio State University, researchers compared the health of 32 separated or divorced men with that of 32 married men. The two groups were carefully matched in economic and occupational circumstances. Nor were the two groups distinguishable by "even marginal differences in health–related behaviors (weight loss, sleep, caffeine intake, and alcohol and cigarette use)." Yet the OSU researchers found that while the married men reported an average of only one-half day of sickness during the past two months, the divorced and separated suffered an average of almost two days of illness during the same period. Remarkably, blood tests revealed "poorer cellular immune system control" among the divorced and separated than among the married.[13]

Researchers at Goteborg University in Sweden have recently reported similar findings based on a much larger study. Looking at the health statistics for about 8,000 middle-aged Swedish men, the GU researchers found a mortality rate of 9 percent among married men over a period of approximately ten years compared with a mortality rate of 20 percent among single men during the same period. The gap in mortality rates could partly be explained as the consequence of differences in health habits, since married men in the study were less likely than the divorced to smoke or to abuse alcohol. Accordingly, "death from alcoholism and liver cirrhosis, as well as suicide and other violent death, were all considerably more common in divorced men" than among the married in this study. Yet even after taking health habits and occupational class into account, the researchers established that "death from causes other than cancer and cardiovascular disease was strongly associated with marital status."[14] These findings deserve particular scrutiny because the Swedish marriage rate is now the lowest in the industrialized world while the Swedish rate of family dissolution is perhaps the highest.[15]

In a study published in 1982, Jukka T. Salonen of the University of Kuopio in Finland examined the health records for over 3,600 middle-aged Finnish men. Even after results were statistically adjusted to account for tobacco use, cholesterol levels, and blood pressure, this Finnish study showed that an unmarried man was more than twice as likely as a married man to suffer from fatal ischemic heart disease, more than twice as likely to suffer an episode of cerebrovascular disease, and more than twice as likely to die due to any disease.[16]

Clearly, the effects of marriage upon health are not limited to any changes that wedlock may cause in health habits. (Harold Morowitz of Yale University concludes that "being divorced and a nonsmoker is slightly less dangerous than smoking a pack or more a day and staying married," adding facetiously that "if a man's marriage is driving him to heavy smoking, he has a delicate statistical decision to make."[17]) Many researchers now explain the health benefits of marriage as a consequence of social support. Evidence from the widely noted longitudinal study in Alameda County, California, suggests that marriage is only one type — albeit a particularly important type — of "social network tie" affecting health. In their analysis of the Alameda County data, researchers for The National Institute for Aging find that marital status assumes "primary importance" in determining mortality rates among those less than 60 years old. However, for older age groups, ties with close friends or relatives appear more important than marriage in determining mortality risk. For these older groups, "the presence of contacts with friends and/or relatives would seem to represent an important protection against increased mortality risk, perhaps even substituting to some extent for the tie with a spouse which is more likely lost at older ages."[18]

In a study published in 1989, Swedish epidemiologists provided new evidence that marriage reduces mortality by providing social support. Comparing their research to the Alameda County Study, the authors of the new Swedish study established "an independent association between marital status and all-cause mortality . . . even though the importance of marital status to mortality seems to decrease with age." The Swedish researchers interpreted the effects of marital status within a broader pattern in which they established an "association between social network, social support, and all-cause mortality."[19]

Social ties also apparently account for the pattern identified by Ofra Anson in a recent analysis of data collected in the National Health Interview Survey. Examining the reported health of over 20,000 white women ages 18 to 55, Anson found that living arrangements are more important to women's health than are age, education, or household income. Single women living alone spend more days sick in bed and suffer more chronic conditions than do women living with husbands. Single women living with unrelated persons likewise suffer worse health than married women, but not as bad as that of singles living alone. "For women who live alone," Anson concludes, "the costs incurred by the absence of steady adult support outweigh the benefits of being independent, having privacy, and freedom from intensive nurturant responsibilities. They are in poorer health than those in all living arrangements that offer adult support." But those women reporting the worst health are unmarried mothers; compared to other groups of women, unmarried mothers visit doctors more often, spend more days sick in bed, and are hospitalized more often. Anson found that two relatively small groups of unmarried women — those who live with their parents or their grown children — actually enjoy better health than married women, evidently because these women enjoy the benefits of adult suppport without bearing the responsibilities of caring for children.[20]

In 1989, researchers at Columbia University published a particularly sophisticated analysis of the health effects of the social support found through marriage. The Columbia researchers classified almost two million deaths occurring in 1986 according to the cause of death and according to the likelihood that such deaths might have been prevented or delayed by "formal" care (the kind of care received from physicians or other professionals), "informal" care (the kind of care received from family members or friends), or some combination of formal and informal care. The results revealed that for both men and women, for both blacks and whites, for almost every age group, marriage provides protection against early death. The protective effect of marriage appeared most pronounced for types of death that can be delayed or prevented chiefly through informal care. Most of the causes of death included in this category were chronic diseases, such as diabetes, cirrhosis, asthma, and hypertensive heart disease. For this category, the mortality rate of unmarried white males ages 35 to 54 ran an astounding 390 percent higher than for their married peers. Among unmarried females, the mortality rate for this type of death ran 200 percent higher than for their married peers. Among white females, the mortality rate for this type of death ran 200 percent higher for unmarrieds ages 35 to 44 and 120 percent higher for unmarrieds 45 to 54, compared to married women of the same ages. A parallel but less dramatic pattern appears among blacks. Mortality rates for this type of death run 265 percent higher for unmarried than for married black men ages 35 to 44, almost 190 percent higher for ages 45 to 54. Among black women, the mortality rate for this type of death runs 110 percent higher for unmarrieds ages 35 to 44, almost 89 percent higher for ages 45 to 54.

Although not quite as stark, the same pattern prevailed for accidental deaths and suicide, for which prevention depends almost entirely upon timely informal care. "Deaths caused by falling asleep in bed with a cigarette or driving when drunk," explain the researchers, "can be prevented by a spouse, who can remove the cigarette or do the driving. Avoiding these hazards requires no technical training but does require . . . long-term commitment and face-to-face contact."

Surprisingly, however, mortality rates ran significantly higher among singles than among marrieds even for types of death (such as those caused by cancer of the gallbladder or by hemorrhage of the subarachnoid artery) which require formal care and which are thought to be little affected by informal care. For deaths in this category, mortality rates still ran significantly higher for unmarried than for married. Among white males, for instance, the unmarried ages 35 to 54 suffered a mortality rate almost 100 percent higher than their married peers. The link between marriage and lower mortality rates appears to be broken only for types of death (such as those caused by cancer of the brain or pancreas) for which little may be done through formal or informal care.[21]

In a recent examination of the relationship between marriage and cancer — the nation's second leading cause of death — epidemiologists at the Michigan Cancer Foundation could find no consistent relationship between cancer and marital status (although a statistical relationship between marriage and lower cancer rates could be discerned for a few specific types of cancer, such as cancer of the buccal cavity among black and white males and among black females; lung cancer among blacks of both sexes; and cervical and ovarian cancer for females of both races). However, the authors of this study did note evidence that "marriage influences survivorship among cancer patients," even if it does not prevent its occurrence.[22] Indeed, in a study conducted in 1987 in New Mexico, researchers found that unmarried victims of cancer are more likely to go untreated for cancer than married victims and even if treated are still less likely to survive than married victims. "The decreases in survival [among cancer victims] associated with being unmarried are not trivial," the researchers noted.[23]

Most of the research on the physical health effects of divorce has focused on adults, not children. But parental divorce does appear to put children's health at risk. In his popular book *The Broken Heart: The Medical Consequences of Loneliness* (1979), James Lynch of the University of Maryland cited evidence that parental divorce not only causes mental neuroses, but also helps foster "various physical diseases, including cardiac disorders" later in their lives.[24] In contrast, in a 1986 study at the Oregon Health Science University, Shirley Hanson found — on the basis of a small sample — that single parenthood does *not* harm children's health.[25] Yet in a study published in 1985, researchers from Kent State University and the University of Akron found that in a national survey children of divorced parents suffered significantly worse health than the children of intact marriages. The authors of the 1985 study concluded that "marital status is related to health status of all the family members including both parents and children." The researchers found evidence that the differences in health reflected differences in "environmental stress."[26]

In 1988, researchers from Rutgers University examined two health surveys conducted by the National Center for Health Statistics, finding that "single mothers report poorer overall physical health for their children." The authors of the Rutgers study explain their finding by noting that many unmarried mothers live in poverty, so exposing their children to greater health risks, and that a disproportionate number of single mothers are young and therefore more likely to bear an illness-prone premature infant. The Rutgers researchers also uncovered evidence that unmarried mothers are more likely than married mothers to exaggerate the health problems of their children.[27] Indeed, Finnish health authorities at the University of Tampere find that children from broken homes are significantly more likely to require medical attention for psychosomatic symptoms than children from intact families.[28]

Like divorce, illegitimacy appears linked to harmful — often fatal — health problems for children. In a study completed in 1987, researchers at the National Center for Health Statistics found that compared with married mothers, unmarried women run "a substantially higher risk of having infants with very low or moderately low birth weights." Low birth weight defines one of the best predictors of infant mortality. The NCHS researchers believe that marriage exerts no "direct causal influence on the outcome of pregnancy," but argue that a life course that includes marriage is likely to be healthier than one that does not. (Unmarried mothers are, for example, more likely to smoke than married mothers.)[29]

Divorce and illegitimacy also affect the future health of children by increasing the likelihood that they will use tobacco. In recent studies in the United States and Canada, researchers have established a significant correlation between broken homes and adolescent use of tobacco.[30]

American policymakers and concerned citizens can hardly ignore the apparent linkage between family dissolution and poor health at a time of high divorce and illegitimacy rates and of low and falling marriage rates. The American divorce rate has risen more than 40 percent since 1970, by almost 250 percent since 1940.[31] More than 40 percent of marriages formed in the 1980's are probably headed for divorce. On the other hand, the rate for first marriages has dropped more than 30 percent since 1970; one American in eight now remains unmarried for life.[32] Partly because of a sharp drop in marital fertility, the proportion of the nation's children born out of wedlock has soared. In 1960, only one birth in twenty was illegitimate. In 1985, almost one birth in four was out of wedlock.[33]

The health costs associated with this national retreat from family life are not only the burden of individual households, but of the taxpayers. Largely because of the rise in illegitimacy, taxpayers now pay the birth costs for one infant in seven. Because illegitimate children are born prematurely with alarming frequency, they often require special surgery, mechanical respirators, isolation incubators, and other costly medical care paid for out of general hospital funds and the public purse. In a 1984 study at the National Center for Health Services Research, analysts found that divorced women were not only less healthy than married women (despite the fact that "the divorced population is somewhat younger than the married"), but that divorced women are more likely than married women to rely on public assistance for health care.[34] Likewise, in their study in 1988 on single motherhood and children's health, researchers at Rutgers commented that unmarried mothers and their children "disproportionately constitute a population which is chronically dependent on the state for basic necessities, including health care."[35]

The erosion of family life not only drives up the nation's future medical bills, it also reduces the number of future taxpayers who can pay those bills. Policy analyst Ben Wattenberg identifies the trend toward fewer, later, and less stable marriages as a primary reason for a national fertility rate which has languished below replacement level for more than a decade.[36] Illegitimate births among unmarried women do not make up for the drop in fertility among married women. Among married women aged 18 to 44 living with their husbands, the birth rate stands at 97 per 1,000, low by historic standards, but still two-and-a-half times higher than the rate of 38.1 per 1,000 unmarried women of the same ages.[37] Fewer births now translates into a smaller tax base in thirty or forty years. Wattenberg indeed believes that the "birth dearth" could cause the Social Security system to fail early in the next century if—as many predict—the Social Security trust fund is combined with the Medicare trust fund.[38]

Family disruption and depressed fertility not only erode the tax base; these developments also create higher public costs for the institutional care of the sick and elderly. In 1977, Lynch warned that Americans were paying "uncounted billions of dollars" to care for divorced and single people who stay in hospitals longer than do married people suffering from the same illnesses.[39] American taxpayers also face rising costs of institutionalizing elderly persons because of childlessness and family dissolution. In a RAND Corporation study published last fall, Peter Morrison warned that trends in American family life would make it difficult to care for the rising number of elderly Americans. He noted that because of high divorce rates, "the care spouses traditionally have provided each other in old age will be far less available" in the decades ahead. The birth dearth will further exacerbate the difficulty of caring for the elderly. "Early next century when baby boomers grow old," Morrison writes, "they will have few adult children to fill the role of caregiver, because they produced so few offspring." And while the working woman's need for paid child care has received a great deal of attention, the plight of the working woman's elderly parents has received less consideration. Pointing out that "by tradition, adult daughters have provided elderly parents with home care," Morrison sees this kind of care disappearing as women move into paid employment.[40] Writing in the *American Journal of Public Health*, researchers from Vanderbilt University anticipated "intergenerational conflict" provoked by the increasing costs of providing nursing-home care for aging Americans without children able or willing to care for them in their homes.[41] In 1986, annual public expenditures for nursing-home care already stood at over $18 billion.[42]

Because of the profound effects of marriage and family life upon health-care costs, the public debate over how to meet those costs cannot proceed very far without addressing these issues. That debate is already heating up. Writing recently in *The New Republic*, Phillip Longman argued that "Medicare is going broke" because of the aging of the population and the declining American birth rate. "Without fundamental changes, Medicare won't be able to meet the needs of today's middle-aged Americans and their children," Longman reasons, warning that under current policies "the trade-off between health care for the young and the old will become increasingly stark and unavoidable."[43] Formerly chief of staff at the White House under President Lyndon Johnson, James R. Jones predicts that unless current trends can be checked, federal spending on health care could consume 20 percent of every American worker's taxable income by the year 2009. Under such a crushing tax burden, younger Americans would find it hard to avoid "a sizable decline in their future standard of living." Jones therefore calls for "no less than rethinking our notion of health care entitlement from the bottom up."[44]

Fundamental rethinking may account for the rediscovery of family responsibilities by some public-health officials. Richard Morse of Kansas State University sees "some movement, at present, to deny welfare or Medicaid to those individuals whose families cannot prove they are unable to perform that responsibility."[45] Alexa K. Stuifbergen of the University of Texas at Austin likewise believes that "policymakers are increasingly looking to the family as a hedge against the rising cost of health care services."[46]

This rediscovery of family responsibility for health care raises vexing questions, however, in our era of "no fault" divorce and stigma-free illegitimacy. If (as many Americans believe) the government should not "impose values" by promoting any particular lifestyle, is it then just to impose the collectivized *costs* of repudiating those values undergirding marriage and child rearing? If the relationships between family life and public health-care costs are acknowledged, how can a modern welfare state avoid political warfare between lifestyles?

The historian Paul Johnson recently offered a hint of the political passions that may be touched off by the health-care crisis when he warned his fellow conservatives that "health policies" may soon define the field of action for adversaries on the left.[47] Perhaps Johnson's fears were stirred by the recent expansion of Medicare to cover "catastrophic health care" or by proposed legislation mandating that all employers provide health care insurance for workers and dependents ("Minimum Health Benefits for All Workers Act of 1987," S. 1265). Congress has since repealed "catastrophic health care," but former U.S. Senator J. William Fulbright would gladly fulfill Johnson's worst nightmares. In 1988, Fulbright asserted that Americans could not justly declare their system of government a success in its competitive struggle with communism until "no one in our country need fear avoidable death or disease for lack of affordable medical care."[48]

Even if achievement of Fulbright's ideal standard for health care were technically feasible, it might not be socially or politically desirable. In the framing of health-care policy, Americans need to ask whether personal freedom or family integrity could survive a utopian assault upon disease. From Plato to B.F. Skinner, utopians have regarded the family as a regressive social unit and therefore an obstacle to the creation of the ideal state. In one of the great anti-utopian novels of this century, *Brave New World* (1932), Aldous Huxley depicted a regime of hedonistic totalitarianism in which the state has conquered sickness — and destroyed the family. In the climactic episode, a "Savage" who has not been programmed by state psychologists protests against a world in which marriage and disease have disappeared together. Dismayed that he cannot marry because marriage has disappeared as an institution, the Savage protests also against the engineered healthiness of the world. "I don't want comfort," the Savage insists. Claiming "the right to be unhappy," the Savage also affirms "the right to grow old and ugly and impotent; the right to have syphilis and cancer; the right to have too little to eat; the right to be lousy; the right to live in constant apprehension of what may happen tomorrow; the right to catch typhoid; the right to be tortured by unspeakable pains."[49]

Some Americans may regard the Savage's tirade against an imaginary utopia as irrelevant to circumstances in the United States. Others will point to evidence that even in its limited attempts to mitigate uncertainty and suffering, the welfare state has weakened family life. In a study conducted in 1986 for the Joint Economic Committee, Congress of the United States, economists Lowell Gallaway and Richard Vedder found that rising Federal public aid has had a "very substantial" effect upon the nation's divorce rate.[50] Although the issue remains controversial, many observers believe that welfare benefits also foster illegitimacy.[51] A former Fulbright scholar in Sweden, a country with an exceptionally well-developed welfare system, David Popenoe has gone so far as to suggest that "the inherent character of the welfare state by its very existence help[s] to undermine family values or familism — the belief in a strong sense of family identification and loyalty, mutual assistance among family members, and a concern for the perpetuation of the family unit." Popenoe points out that although many of Sweden's welfare programs "began with the goal of helping families to function better," over time "the very acceleration of welfare-state power weakened the family still further."[52]

To the degree that American policymakers expand the health services available from the welfare state, they likewise run the risk of weakening the family. Anthropologists Glynn Custred and Andrei Simic note the "circular relationships . . . in which the state is increasingly called upon to fill the void created by the erosion of the family's primary functions, and in so doing further aggravates the situation."[53] In pointing to what might be taken as an example of this "circular relationship," Stephen Crystal documents the difficulty federal officials have encountered in trying to reverse a previous policy of paying the nursing-home costs of elderly parents with adult children. Though financially able children once covered such costs, many affluent Americans now resist the notion that they are responsible for their aging parents. "It's hard," observes Crystal, "to unscramble an omelet."[54]

No easy resolution to the health care crisis appears possible. Marriage and family life foster good health; yet, Americans are in retreat from family life. In any case, Americans rarely choose to accept or avoid the commitments of marriage and family in order to control their health-care costs. If Aldous Huxley saw clearly, then the capacity to make family ties actually requires a willingness to accept risks, including health risks. Even the development of private, nongovernment forms of health insurance may signal a movement away from reliance upon the family. Social historians locate the origins of insurance companies in "the passage from the predominant rural *Gemeinschaft*, close-knit eighteenth-century community to a more impersonal and urbanized *Gesellschaft* type of society." As historian Douglas C. North observes:

> The self-sufficiency of the family unit in an agricultural and domestic economy gave way to the economic interdependence of an industrial capitalist order. . . . The creation of a large section of the population without property and dependent on a money income . . . resulted in family insecurity. . . . Insurance was a contrivance to mitigate this insecurity.[55]

America's retreat from family life is the consequence of many diverse cultural trends, most of them beyond the direct control of policymakers in a liberal democracy. American government officials are now asked to cope with the rising medical costs created by family dissolution; yet, by collectivizing those costs, these officials help cause further erosion of family ties. It is a dilemma sure to unsettle the nation in the decades ahead.

—*Bryce J. Christensen is director of The Rockford Institute Center on The Family in America.*

ENDNOTES

[1]Bureau of the Census, *Statistical Abstract of the United States: 1989*, 109th ed. (Washington: U.S. Government Printing Office, 1988), p. 92.

[2]James R. Jones, "Aging and Generational Equity: When Past, Present and Future Converge," *The Internist*, January 1989, p. 6.

[3]Bureau of the Census, *Statistical Abstract of the United States: 1989*, p. 92.

[4]Jones, "Aging and Generational Equity," p. 7.

[5]Catherine K. Riessman and Naomi Gerstel, "Marital Dissolution and Health: Do Males or Females Have Greater Risk?" *Social Science and Medicine* 20 (1985):627.

[6]Charlotte A. Schoenborn and Barbara F. Wilson, "Are Married People Healthier? Health Characteristics of Married and Unmarried U.S. Men and Women," paper presented at the American Public Health Association, Boston, Massachusetts, 15 November 1988, pp. 3, 4, 9, 15.

[7]Sigismund Peller, "Studies on Mortality Since the Renaissance," *Bulletin of the History of Medicine* 13 (1943):435-441 and 21 (1947):73-99.

[8]William Farr, "Marriage and Mortality," in *Vital Statistics: A Memorial Volume of Selections from the Reports and Writings of William Farr* (London, 1885; rpt. Metuchen, N.J.: The Library of the New York Academy of Medicine/The Scarecrow Press, 1975), pp. 438-441.

[9]Ellen E. Kisker and Noreen Goldman, "Perils of Single Life and Benefits of Marriage," *Social Biology* 34 (1987):135-140.

[10]Joseph Berkson, "Mortality and Marital Status: Reflections on the Derivation of Etiology from Statistics," *American Journal of Public Health* 52 (1962):1318-1329.

[11]Debra Umberson, "Family Status and Health Behaviors: Social Control as a Dimension of Social Integration," *Journal of Health and Social Behavior* 28 (1987):309-316.

[12]John A. Clausen, "Health and the Life Course: Some Personal Observations," *Journal of Health and Social Behavior* 28 (1987):337-344.

[13]Janice K. Kiecolt-Glaser *et al.*, "Marital Discord and Immunity in Males," *Psychosomatic Medicine* 50 (1988):213-229.

[14]Annika Rosengren, Hans Wedel, and Lars Wilhelmsen, "Medical Status and Mortality in Middle-Aged Swedish Men," *American Journal of Epidemiology* 129 (1989):54-63.

[15]See David Popenoe, "What Is Happening to the Family in Sweden?" *Social Change in Sweden*, No. 36, Swedish Information Service, December 1986, pp. 1-7.

[16]Jukka T. Salonen, "Socioeconomic status and risk of cancer, cerebral stroke, and death due to coronary heart disease and any disease: a longitudinal study in eastern Finland," *Journal of Epidemiology and Community Health* 36 (1987):294-297.

[17]Morowitz quoted by James L. Lynch in *The Broken Heart: The Medical Consequences of Loneliness* (New York: Basic, 1977), pp. 45-46.

[18]Teresa E. Seeman *et al.*, "Social Network Ties and Mortality Among the Elderly in the Alameda County Study," *American Journal of Epidemiology* 126 (1987):714-721.

[19]Bertil S. Hanson *et al.*, "Social Network and Social Support Influence Mortality in Elderly Men," *American Journal of Epidemiology* 130 (1989):100-111.

[20]Ofra Anson, "Living Arrangements and Women's Health," *Social Science and Medicine* 26 (1988):201-208.

[21]Eugene Litwak *et al.*, "Organizational Theory, Social Supports, and Mortality Rates: A Theoretical Convergence," *American Sociological Review* 54 (1989):49-66.

[22]G. Marie Swanson, Steven H. Belle, and William A. Satariano, "Marital Status and Cancer Incidence: Differences in the Black and White Populations," *Cancer Research* 45 (1985):5883-5889.

[23]James S. Goodwin *et al.*, "The Effect of Marital Status on Stage, Treatment, and Survival of Cancer Patients," *Journal of the American Medical Association* 258 (1987):3125-3130.

[24]Lynch, *The Broken Heart*, pp. 78-80.

[25]Shirley M.H. Hanson, "Healthy Single Parent Families," *Family Relations* 35 (1986):125-132.

[26]John Guidubaldi and Helen Cleminshaw, "Divorce, Family Health, and Child Adjustment," *Family Relations* 34 (1985):35-41.

[27]Ronald Angel and Jacqueline L. Worobey, "Single Motherhood and Children's Health," *Journal of Health and Social Behavior* 29 (1988):38-52.

[28]Hilleui Aro *et al.*, "Psychosomatic Symptoms Among 14-16 Year Old Finnish Adolescents," *Social Psychiatry* 22 (1987):171-176.

[29]Joel C. Kleinman and Samuel S. Kessel, "Racial Differences in Low Birth Weight," *New England Journal of Medicine* 317 (1987):749-753.

[30]See Rhys B. Jones and D. Paul Moberg, "Correlates of Smokeless Tobacco Use in a Male Adolescent Population," *American Journal of Public Health* 78 (1988):61-63; Jean-Francois Saucier and Ann-Marie Ambert, "Parental Marital Status and Adolescents' Health-Risk Behavior," *Adolescence* 18 (1983):403-411.

[31]Bureau of the Census, *Statistical Abstract of the United States: 1989*, p. 85; Bureau of the Census, *Historical Statistics of the United States: Colonial Times to 1970* (Washington: U.S. Government Printing Office, 1976), 1:64.

[32]Robert Schoen, "The Continuing Retreat From Marriage: Figures From 1983 U.S. Marital Status Life Tables," *Sociology and Social Research* 71 (1987):108-109; Bureau of the Census, *Statistical Abstract of the United States: 1989*, p. 85.

[33]Bureau of the Census, *Statistical Abstract of the United States: 1989*, p. 66.

[34]Marc L. Berk and Amy K. Taylor, "Women and Divorce: Health Insurance Coverage, Utilization, and Health Care Expenditures," *American Journal of Public Health* 74 (1984):1276-1279.

[35]Angel and Worobey, "Single Motherhood and Children's Health," p. 49.

[36]Ben J. Wattenberg, *The Birth Dearth* (New York: Pharos, 1987), pp. 124-126.

[37]Bureau of the Census, *Statistical Abstract of the United States: 1989*, p. 67.

[38]Wattenberg, *The Birth Dearth*, pp. 68-70.

[39]Lynch, *The Broken Heart*, p. 209.

[40]Peter A. Morrison, "The Current Demographic Context of Federal Social Programs," N-2785-HHS/NICHD, The RAND Corporation, September 1988, pp. 9-12.

[41]Wayne A. Ray *et al.*, "Impact of Growing Numbers of the Very Old on Medicaid Expenditures for Nursing Homes: A Multi-State, Population-Based Analysis," *American Journal of Public Health* 77 (1987):699-703.

[42]Bureau of the Census, *Statistical Abstract of the United States: 1989*, p. 94.

[43]Phillip Longman, "Deathbed Politics," *The New Republic*, 30 March 1987, pp. 18-20.

[44]Jones, "Aging and Generational Equity," p. 8.

[45]"Interview: Richard L.D. Morse, Ph.D.," *Family and Community Health* 9 (February 1987):85.

[46]Alexa K. Stuifbergen, "The Impact of Chronic Illness on Families," *Family and Community Health* 9 (February 1987):50.

[47]Paul Johnson, "Is Totalitarianism Dead? New Temptations for Today's Intellectuals," *Crisis*, February 1989, p. 16.

[48]J. William Fulbright and Seth P. Tillman, "Our new opportunity to beat swords into plow shares," *Chicago Tribune*, 19 April 1989, Sec. 1, p. 13.

[49]Aldous Huxley, *Brave New World* (1932; rpt. New York: Harper & Row, 1969), pp. 160-163.

[50]Lowell Gallaway and Richard Vedder, *Poverty, Income Distribution, the Family and Public Policy*, a Study prepared for the use of the Subcommittee on Trade, Productivity, and Economic Growth of the Joint Economic Committee, Congress of the United States, December 19, 1986 (Washington: U.S. Government Printing Office, 1986), pp. 84-89.

[51]See Nathan Glazer, *The Limits of Social Policy* (Cambridge: Harvard University Press, 1988), pp. 18-33.

[52]David Popenoe, *Disturbing the Nest: Family Change and Decline in Modern Societies* (New York: Aldine de Gruyter, 1988), pp. 237-239.

[53]Glynn Custred and Andrei Simic, "Modernity and the American Family: A Cultural Dilemma," *International Journal of the Sociology of the Family* 12 (1982):163.

[54]Stephen Crystal, *America's Old Age Crisis: Public Policy and the Two Worlds of Aging* (New York: Basic, 1982), p. 13.

[55]See Viviana A.R. Zelizer, *Morals and Markets: The Development of Life Insurance in the United States* (New York: Columbia University Press, 1979), p. 12.

Conference on The Social Costs of Family Dissolution Clock Tower Inn, Rockford, Illinois

October 13-14, 1989

Chairman
Douglas Besharov
Resident Scholar
American Enterprise Institute

Authors of Papers
Sarah McLanahan
Professor of Sociology
University of Wisconsin

Armand M. Nicholi, Jr., M.D.
Associate Clinical Professor of Psychiatry
Harvard Medical School

Travis Hirschi
Professor of Public Policy
University of Arizona

Bryce Christensen
Director
The Rockford Institute Center on The Family in America

Participants
Carl Anderson
Vice President of Public Policy
Knights of Columbus
Washington, D.C.

Allan Carlson
President
The Rockford Institute

Stephen Chapman
Editorial Board
Chicago Tribune

William Donohue
Professor of Sociology
LaRoche College

Charles A. Donovan
Deputy Director of Government Relations
Family Research Council

Marilyn Gardner
Christian Science Monitor
Boston, Massachusetts

Victor Gecas
Professor of Sociology
Washington State University

Gordon Jones
D G M International
Burke, Virginia

Steven Nock
Professor of Sociology
University of Virginia

J. Craig Peery
Professor of Human Development
Brigham Young University

Robert Sampson
Professor of Sociology
University of Illinois

Richard Vedder
Professor of Economics
Ohio University

Family Failure — Summary of a Discussion

Sociologist and psychiatrist, economist and journalist, attorney and historian — although divided by profession, the seventeen people who gathered in October 1989 at the Clock Tower Inn in Rockford, Illinois, were united in their concern about "The Social Costs of Family Dissolution." As conference participants considered the four papers published in this volume, their lively discussion opened onto many topics not directly addressed in the papers.

Presenting the first paper of the conference, Professor Armand Nicholi, Jr. remarked upon the irony of the government's recent declaration of war on drugs. It is as naive for Americans to suppose that the drug war is new as it would have been for Europeans during the 1940's to have resisted the reality of World War II until their cities were devastated. Nicholi recalled his early experiences with the drug war back in the early 1960's when he had just completed his medical training. Working at Harvard, he had wondered why young people who placed such a high premium on their intellectual function would take drugs that could and often did seriously impair their mental faculties, even send them to mental hospitals. At the same time that he was investigating student drug use, Nicholi was also researching the backgrounds of students who dropped out of Harvard University. Among students who had dropped out of the University for emotional reasons, he discovered that a disproportionate number had early in their lives lost a parent through death. Pursuing the matter further, Nicholi began to realize that death is only one of the ways a child may lose a parent. Children may also lose parents through divorce, through emotional illness, or through time-demanding jobs. Nicholi reported that among the young men with psychiatric problems at Harvard, many had highly successful but absent fathers. Viewing their fathers as cold, distant, and critical, these troubled young men often suffered from identity problems which they tried to resolve through a passion for sports cars and motorcycles — often leading to serious accidents, including a significant number of paralyzing back injuries.

During about the same era — the 1960's — when he was uncovering these relationships between mental health and family

life, Nicholi observed a significant change in child-rearing practices, as a growing number of parents began to relegate care to
agencies outside of the home. Other investigators at the time found
that American parents were spending less time with their children
than parents in any other country. Such developments, Nicholi
believed, were causally linked to the rise of the drug culture. People
who take drugs typically manifest distinctive personality traits,
including low self-esteem, despondency, and rejection of authority.
Research revealed that children from broken homes were more
vulnerable to drug use than children from intact homes. It is no
accident that the incidence of drug use paralleled the divorce rate,
both rising rapidly in the late 1960's. "If we know anything about
how the human mind develops," Nicholi stressed, "it is that a child
needs a close, warm, sustained relationship with both parents."
The absence of such relationships may contribute to a variety of
emotional disorders.

Underscoring the importance of parental ties, Nicholi noted the
persistence of the fear of abandonment, a fear distressing alike new
infants and dying adults. This fear appears to be both the first and
last of fears, pervading all of our lives. Coping with this fear has
grown more difficult for children who see less and less of their
parents. In the past, fathers were present in the family too little.
But instead of bringing them back into family life, Americans have
sent mothers out into the workplace with fathers, making spouses
emotionally less accessible to one another and making parents less
emotionally accessible to their children. The consequences include
not only a higher divorce rate, but also a feeling of rejection among
many children. Among children who experience it, this feeling of
rejection breeds anger. If the child turns this anger and resentment
inward, the result is often depression of the sort now seen in a
distressing number of young people. If children turn their anger at
being rejected outward rather than inward, they express that
anger by acting out, often becoming involved in violence and crime.

Nicholi marveled that despite these massive problems and the
evidence of their causes, few public figures say anything about
strengthening families. Those who do speak out against divorce or
in favor of parental commitment to children often find themselves
accused of trying to turn back the clock, of being primitive and
atavistic.

In his prepared response to Professor Nicholi's paper, Professor Victor Gecas noted that he spoke from a sociological perspective that differs from Dr. Nicholi's clinical perspective. Gecas observed that family dissolution has actually been increasing since the turn of the century, though the rate has accelerated since the 1960's. The rising abuse of drugs in recent decades not only parallels the rise in divorce, but it also remarkably parallels the rate of women's employment, especially among married women. Gecas agreed that the key issue in family dissolution may be how divorce or illegitimacy affects the conditions in which children are raised and live. This issue is important to any consideration of the continuity or health of society.

Yet Gecas expressed far less certainty than Nicholi about the consequences of family dissolution. He questioned whether family dissolution and its consequences — i.e., one-parent families, stepfamilies — necessarily cause a lack of nurturance and support for children. The research that Nicholi cites in his paper consists largely of clinical studies focused on small non-representative samples of largely troubled individuals. When sociologists perform studies with larger, more representative samples, they discover a more equivocal, less clear-cut picture of the consequences of family dissolution than that provided in Nicholi's paper. Gecas found more questions than answers in recent research on how family dissolution affects children, pointing to the need for greater precision and specificity than Nicholi had provided in his discussion of children's problems. For instance, Gecas noted that while children of divorced parents appear to have more academic problems than children from intact homes, the outcomes of parental divorce appear less clear for psychological and emotional development. Such outcomes apparently vary according to the age and sex of the child of the divorcing parents. Gecas cautioned conference participants not to rely on sweeping generalizations, but rather to attend to specific issues.

Gecas identified the loss of income associated with family dissolution and all that this implies — e.g., lowered standard of living, greater need for maternal employment, moving to a new neighborhood and new school — as one of the major mechanisms for the negative consequences of divorce on child development. A major problem with many of the studies on family dissolution is that they fail to take social class and downward economic mobility into account. Is it primarily father's absence or loss of father's income that affects child development in mother-only families? Gecas asked.

Gecas also drew attention to the problem of causal inference in studies on the effects of family dissolution. Most such studies are based on cross-sectional designs, whereas longitudinal research is needed to answer some of these questions. Is it (for example) divorce per se that has negative consequences for children, or is it mainly the family conflict, tension, and poor family relations often associated with families that divorce (so that if some of these troubled families stay together the consequences for the children may be just as bad)?

Convinced that the best one-parent family could not begin to compare to a healthy intact family, William Donohue blamed the upsurge in divorce upon the emergence in the 1960's and 1970's of a false new definition of freedom as unlimited rights without responsibilities. Americans are now paying a high price for this new freedom, he asserted.

Sidestepping the sociological question, Bryce Christensen voiced fears about the moral and cultural effects of divorce. After all, whatever else a divorce may do, it makes a lie out of wedding vows which pledge union until death. What, he asked, are the consequences for children and for society as a whole of seeing almost half of all wedding vows — vows pronounced publicly and with solemnity — turned into lies?

When discussion turned to a more concrete question of how to curtail divorce, Douglas Besharov reported that his personal experience with men contemplating divorce suggested that property-division laws can exert a powerful deterring effect against divorce, especially in long-term marriages. On the other hand, divorced husbands now usually bear relatively light burdens for child support or spousal support. Noting the existence of horribly abusive marriages, Besharov asked all participants to consider what advice might be given to couples thinking about divorce if they have children.

Robert Sampson remarked that many children of divorced parents come from families severely troubled before the divorce. Given the reality of domestic violence, especially the abuse of children, he thought it overly simplistic to just emphasize the value of families while glossing over this problem. Many of the problems statistically linked to divorce may actually be traced to conflicts that existed prior to divorce. It is not clear that these problems would go away if divorce were eliminated.

Offering a differing perspective, Steven Nock cited research finding that virtually all children react to parental divorce with shock and surprise. Apparently, no matter how bitter the spousal disputes, the children still perceive their relationships as rather warm and loving, even on the eve of divorce.

Children's naiveté about divorce will not last, predicted Gordon Jones, if contemporary literature for children is any indication. It seemed to him that half the books his daughter was bringing home from the library were about the children of divorced parents. Jones expressed misgivings about the apparent effort to educate children to the fact that perhaps their parents' marriage is not permanent.

The emotional risks of exposing children to divorce appeared particularly noticeable to Besharov when an apparently happy neighbor family breaks up. For some time after such a divorce, all the children in the neighborhood feel uncertain and threatened, fearing their own home might break up.

Allan Carlson identified this ripple effect of divorce as strong evidence that divorce is not merely a private decision. Divorce causes reverberations throughout the neighborhood, the extended family, the community. Carlson thought couples contemplating divorce needed to be reminded of the old cliché "You stay together for the sake of the children." Indeed, much of social science amounts to a costly rediscovery of clichés, in Carlson's opinion. In any case, it probably was not social science which brought about the divorce revolution of recent decades. Supported by judges eager to escape the burdens of traditional divorce proceedings, "no fault" divorce won passage in the giddy atmosphere of liberation so dominant during the 1960's and 70's. Other than the Roman Catholic Church, which put up a token opposition in almost every state, no one really opposed "no fault" divorce. Although he acknowledged a long history of rising divorce rates in America, Carlson nonetheless judged the explosion of divorces in the 1960's and 70's as unprecedented, a symptom of a broader social malaise.

Charles Donovan despaired of determining the effects of divorce with any great precision, since no social scientist could ever follow the same family across two contrary choices.

Nicholi lamented that professionals in academic and medical life have typically regarded the family as no more than "a necessary evil" to be attended to as little as possible so that energies can be focused on things judged truly important. Recognizing the importance of the family will require a complete change in attitude. Americans need to realize that the family provides our most significant human experiences, fostering our self-esteem, defining our concept of authority, shaping our entire world view. Nicholi expressed personal satisfaction at the benefits he had enjoyed because of his decision early in his career to devote time every day to his marriage and children. Of course, conflicts sometimes disrupt every family, but Nicholi could see relatively little willingness among many contemporary couples to tolerate the stress of working through such conflict. Rather than resolve their differences with their spouses, many people today immediately form another relationship with someone else who seems to appreciate them more. Soon they see a lawyer, and then it is all over. Yet a year after the event, most divorced couples feel they have made a mistake. The consequences are terrible, especially for children, many of whom experience serious problems in stepfamilies. But beyond the need to avoid divorce, Nicholi saw a need for radical change in attitude among parents, who need to learn to make their children their highest priority. He puzzled over the attitudes of parents who would not hesitate to give their lives for their children if it really came down to that, who nonetheless hesitate to sacrifice even a part of their career for their children.

Citing Emile Durkheim, Travis Hirschi argued that the *possibility* of divorce causes unhappiness in marriage. Reasoning by analogy, he noted that the professors who are unhappy in a department are those with prospects of a job elsewhere, while the people who are stuck get along quite well. Despite the incredulity of Nock and Gecas, Hirschi conjectured that everyone would be happier with marriage if divorce were outlawed.

In skeptical rejoinder, Nock pointed out that Ronald Reagan signed the first "no fault" divorce law in California in 1970 not because he was persuaded of its merits, but because "no fault" divorce was already a reality in the courts. Through chicanery and charades, lawyers and judges routinely sidestepped the formal requirements of adversarial divorce laws. Nock interpreted the history of "no fault" divorce as strong evidence that laws and public policies exert relatively little influence over family life and that therefore it is a mistake to look to the government for a resolution to current family woes.

But Hirschi's view received support from Sara McLanahan, who believed that many marriages are failing precisely because there is an opportunity to break up and because people think that breaking up is going to solve their problems. Accordingly, she thought the state could do something — perhaps not outlaw divorce, but make it much more costly than it is now. As one attempt to dispel the false notion — widespread in the 1970's — that divorce imposes few costs, this conference could help create support for tougher divorce laws governing community-property and child-support settlements. Most studies have found that children from conflict-filled intact families do just as poorly as children of divorced parents; yet, McLanahan wondered whether the parents in the troubled intact family might not have been so unhappy if parents had not been plagued by doubts about whether they should divorce.

Although not wholly unsympathetic to the idea of making divorce harder, Stephen Chapman feared that unless the sexual revolution was somehow repealed, tougher divorce laws might actually make it more attractive for people not to marry in the first place. Addressing himself to Nicholi and Donohue, Chapman wanted to know in what cases divorce would be advisable for parents with children.

Nicholi acknowledged that in some cases divorce is the lesser of two evils after a husband and wife have made a good effort at reconciliation and yet are still destroying one another. Too often, though, the sequence of events leading to divorce looks quite different. Nicholi complained that many couples do not attempt reconciliation. Rather, in a state of anger, many prematurely consult a lawyer, so adopting an irretrievably adversarial posture.

In agreement with Nicholi, Donohue took exception to contemporary arguments justifying divorce on the grounds that one-parent families might enjoy some beneficial advantages. The virtual disappearance of the term "broken family" indicates a deplorable preference for sugar-coating rather than honesty. Himself reared in a broken family, Donohue declared that it would not have made him feel any better as a child if his teachers had avoided the term "broken family." There simply is no substitute for the two-parent family, he reiterated.

For the record, Richard Vedder emphatically took exception to Nock's assertion that conservatives and liberals agree that public policy has had relatively little impact on family life. Beyond the adoption of "no fault" divorce laws, government has taken a number of actions which have profoundly affected homelife. For example, much of the rise in female labor-force participation may be traced to changes in public policy.

Reverting to the debate over the effects of divorce, Christensen cited a 1988 study which found more behavioral problems among children in single-parent households than in intact families in which the parents reported an unsatisfactory marriage. This pattern persisted even when differences in income were taken into account.

Sampson protested against the narrow focus on divorce. After all, a large proportion of children in single-parent households are the offspring of parents who never married. Particularly in the black community, the number of female-headed households reflects not divorce so much as a low marriage rate, itself traceable to the relative scarcity of employed males, skewed sex ratios, and the relatively high incarceration of black males. Policies designed to discourage divorce would not address the problems of women bearing children out of wedlock.

Marilyn Gardner entered the discussion to express dismay at a casual acceptance of divorce among elite men, manifest in a recent article in *Fortune* magazine on "trophy wives," the beautiful, blonde, successful wives that middle-aged executives marry after dumping their matronly first wives who bore their children.

Tongue in cheek, Carlson proposed the imposition of a hefty "divorce tax" on the assets of divorcing couples. Why divorce-crazy Hollywood alone could balance the federal budget under this scheme! he joked. Since government ends up picking up the social debris scattered by divorce, a tax on divorce would not lack justification — even if it lacks political feasibility. Besides, a new tax might serve as a deterrent to divorce. On the other hand, Carlson ruefully conceded that if divorce started to generate tax revenue, government officials might actually start encouraging it, just as they now promote state-sponsored gambling.

Speaking as an attorney, Carl Anderson identified two reasons for making divorce more difficult. First, "no fault" divorce is an extraordinarily radical proposition that lies outside of American legal tradition. "No fault" divorce has helped foment a revolution in family laws. One legal textbook now describes marriage not as a status assumed for life, but as a "speculative joint venture." "No fault" divorce has helped effect a "radical change of expectation" among marrying couples. "No fault" divorce encourages people to concentrate on the individual development of career, while discouraging self-sacrifice to strengthen the marital union. Anderson's second reason for tightening divorce law is that, in cases where couples have children, divorce not only terminates a marriage, but it also splits up a family. "No fault" divorce gives children no rights for the preservation of their home. Although he resisted the notion that marriage is merely a contract, Anderson thought children should be given at least the kind of legal consideration usually given to third-party beneficiaries to a contract, who may demand its enforcement.

But Besharov reminded other conference participants that whatever its economic benefits, traditional family life did entail unequal relationships between men and women. Contemporary family problems spring in part from efforts to shift those relationships. But in this shifting, Americans have neutralized many of the economic benefits that used to accrue to family life. Besharov sensed a need for public policies that would make it more worthwhile for people to marry and have children.

Nock underscored the importance of the benefits of marriage, pointing out that the historical evidence does not support the notion that making divorce costlier will reduce its incidence. Not all states adopted "no fault" divorce at the same time: some adjacent states differed by as much as 5 or 6 years in the adoption of such statutes, yet their divorce rates were virtually the same. Only in New York City does the adoption of "no fault" laws appear to have driven up divorce rates—and even there, the effect appears short-lived. Skeptical of government's power to alter fundamental human attitudes, Nock nonetheless regarded marriage and divorce laws as symbolically important expressions of what family life should mean. "No fault" divorce redefines marriage as simply a contract between two individuals. But in Nock's view, "no fault" divorce was no more than a response to a redefinition of marriage that had already taken place in the broader culture.

Jones still believed that family life offers economic benefits (after all, his children do bring in $15,000 annually delivering the *Washington Post*). However, such benefits have diminished since the time when children typically milked cows, hoed beets, and performed other economically necessary tasks. Married men still earn more money than unmarried men, more than married or unmarried women, suggesting that employers perhaps still think of the needs of the family unit rather than simply those of the atomistic individual. But egalitarian redistributionists have increasingly restricted employers' discretion in recognizing the family obligations of employees, so weakening the sanctions favoring the intact family. The contemporary refusal to stigmatize illegitimate children or divorced men and women also lowers the social costs of family dissolution.

Uneasy with all the talk about the economic benefits of marriage and the costs of divorce, Nicholi stressed that marriages are primarily human relationships. It bothered Nicholi that higher education often conveyed the notions that family is not important and that women who devote themselves to being wives and mothers are second-class citizens. If the Old and New Testaments have anything to teach, it is that our relationships with others define the meaning of our brief time on earth. The two great commandments in Scripture are both about relationships. Nicholi identified the quality of our relationships as the best barometer of our emotional health.

Donohue marveled that illegitimacy is much more prevalent today than it was thirty years ago, even though in 1959 the pill was not commercially available, abortion was illegal, and sex education did not exist. Why has illegitimacy risen even as the technical means to curtail it have grown more available? During the 1950's, illegitimacy and divorce were still occasions for fear, guilt, shame, and ostracism. As Americans have grown more tolerant of diversity, more compassionate toward people with problems, we have lowered the social penalties for family dissolution. On all sorts of questions, Americans increasingly want to discard the stick and use only the carrot. Donohue was not hopeful about the consequences of this one-sided thinking.

Gecas protested against the arguments for making divorce more difficult. In his opinion, people do not go into divorce lightly; rather, for most people who divorce, the decision entails anguish and self-torture. Instead of making divorce tougher, maybe public officials should make marriage tougher, perhaps through some premarital certification test. It makes no sense, Gecas reasoned, to let people marry on a whim, then clobber them when it turns out that their marriage was a mistake.

Historically, marriage and divorce cannot be understood without considering religion, Carlson ventured, noting that not many centuries ago, the churches, not the state, governed marriage and divorce. Yet in recent years, American religious bodies — Protestant and Catholic — have largely lost control of family life. On the other hand, government can markedly shift popular attitudes toward marriage. Carlson noted, for instance, that when Sweden's socialist feminists succeeded in eliminating the joint income tax return — so removing one of the last economic benefits from marriage — marriage rates plummeted. Today, marriage has lost its institutional status in Sweden, so that childbearing is increasingly nonmarital.

Sweden looked different to McLanahan, who insisted on the distinction between marriage and parenting. The marriage rate may be declining in Sweden, but over half of unmarried fathers still live with their children and the unmarried mothers. This is not what is happening in the United States.

McLanahan began the second session by summarizing the themes of her paper. She acknowledged the remarkable growth in the number of single-parent families since 1960, yet she emphasized that family disruption is not a new thing. The percentage of children — white and black — not living with both parents was almost the same in 1900 as it was in 1970. But whereas children formerly lost parents through death, since 1970 the divorce rate has surpassed the death rate as a cause of family dissolution. Based on the most recent projections, demographers now predict that half of all children born in the last ten years will live in a single-parent family before they reach age 18. This trend is not just a woman's problem; it is everyone's problem. McLanahan painted a bleak picture of the economic status of unmarried mothers. About 50 percent of such mothers live below the official poverty line — a statistic that has changed little since 1970. The government has done more for its elderly (whose poverty rate has dropped from about 33 percent to 13 percent since 1970) than it has done for single mothers with children.

An unmarried mother finds herself handicapped, McLanahan explained, in her dependence upon three sources of income: her own earnings; the contributions of the father who no longer lives in the home; and the benefits from the state. Not only do unmarried mothers receive lower wages than men, they must cope with heavier responsibilities for child care than most men bear. Unmarried fathers pay relatively little or nothing in child support. While the government offers a generous program (Survivors' Insurance) for widowed mothers, mothers who are divorced or have never married receive low benefits from the state and can qualify for these benefits only if they are poor.

Enumerating a number of negative consequences of being reared in a single-parent household, McLanahan saw evidence refuting the notion (widespread in the 1970's) that divorce imposed no serious costs on children. In research since 1982 based on national longitudinal data, she discovered a strong statistical correlation between being reared in a single-parent household and dropping out of high school, bearing an illegitimate child during adolescence, and being unemployed in young adulthood. These statistical relationships held consistent across almost all race and ethnic groups, including blacks, whites, Native Americans, Mexican Americans and Puerto Ricans. Asian Americans appear to be the only group among whom single parenthood does not appear to entail these negative consequences, perhaps because they have extremely low rates of single parenthood. McLanahan further qualified her generalizations by noting that on average the children of widowed mothers are doing somewhat better than the children of unmarried mothers. Indeed, on some measures, the children of widowed mothers appear indistinguishable from children living with both parents. Perhaps surprisingly, the children of never-married parents do not appear to be worse off than the children of divorced or separated parents. Nor are children living with unmarried fathers doing appreciably better or worse than children living with unmarried mothers. Boys and girls seem equally at risk for adverse long-term consequences from being reared in a single-parent household. Finally, remarriage of an unmarried parent does not seem to help the children involved, even though it improves their economic circumstances. In statistical profile, children living in stepfamilies look much like children of unmarried parents in their propensity to drop out of school, bear an illegitimate child, or to be unemployed during young adulthood.

McLanahan outlined three possible explanations for the adverse consequences of being reared in a single-parent household. First, some of the problems of children from single-parent homes may be traced to the low income of such households, but McLanahan estimated that the disparity in income could only explain about 25 to 50 percent of the gap separating children of unmarried parents from the children of married parents. Second, single-parent households do not socialize their children the same way two-parent households socialize their children. Teaching children values is harder for unmarried parents than for married parents. Third, children in single-parent families are more likely than children in intact families to live in bad neighborhoods, so exposing them to more difficult environments. Some researchers theorize that the problem lies not with the community or neighborhood that single-parent families live in, but rather with the quality of those families' attachments to the community. McLanahan noted that divorce typically requires a move and the establishment of new community ties.

Investigators generally believe that many of the problems of children in single-parent households can be traced to problems in the family prior to the divorce, so that the divorce itself has not caused the problems. Yet in McLanahan's view, divorce *per se* entails some negative effects for children. Because of these negative effects, policymakers face a major dilemma: they can act either to *prevent* children from living in single-parent households; or they can *alleviate* the economic hardships of children living in single-parent households. Policymakers could reduce the hardship of single-parent households by ensuring higher income for such households and by helping to provide job placement and child care. These policies would probably increase the number of such households. Maternal employment in single-parent households could also hurt children, depending on the quality and effects of day care. Policies that increase the difficulty of divorce giving parents reason to think twice or three times before divorcing might include provision for higher child-support payments from divorced fathers, while at the same time giving those fathers more access to their children, so increasing the cost of divorce for mothers. Such anti-divorce policies would curtail individual freedom and privacy and might be impossible to enforce in some cases.

McLanahan hoped that policymakers might strike a balance between their efforts to curb the divorce rate and their measures to reduce the harmful economic effects of divorce on children. In any case, she felt the time was past for a casual attitude toward divorce.

Vedder commended McLanahan for providing a useful and generally perceptive analysis of the adverse economic effects of family dissolution. He particularly underscored McLanahan's observation that the welfare system creates very severe work disincentives for mother-only families. If welfare is considered as a form of negative income taxation, then it may be truly said that the marginal rate of income taxation for work is far higher on low-income welfare recipients than on any other group in the country — except perhaps the elderly. Vedder could think of no plausible justification for a social policy that discourages work among the welfare population and among senior citizens. Impressed and sobered by McLanahan's evidence on the harm to children caused by divorce, Vedder expressed concerns about her discussion of the policy implications of such harm. He wondered about McLanahan's aversion to policies making divorce more costly, especially since she herself points out that programs for reducing the economic hardship of mother-only families (through larger welfare payments, rigorous collection of child support, accommodations for child care, and subsidies for working mothers' earnings) may actually increase the incidence of divorce, thereby exposing more children to the noneconomic harms of divorce. He complained that — as in most studies dealing with mother-only families — McLanahan's paper failed to discuss why divorce and illegitimacy have risen so much during the past 20 years. Although these trends partly reflect the declining influence of religion and changing gender roles in society, Vedder blamed government for creating new incentives fostering divorce and illegitimacy. Welfare, Medicaid, food stamps, and housing subsidies markedly reduced the economic cost of illegitimacy in recent decades, while the federal government's inflationary macroeconomic policies caused massive unanticipated inflation, so straining household finances and often causing family breakups. New tax credits for child care, made more valuable by the rise in income-tax rates during the 1970's, accelerated the trend toward two-earner families, even as the value of tax deductions for dependent children declined. Such government policies hastened the erosion of the traditional economic basis of marriage, namely that wives exchanged household services for the income security provided by their husbands. Government has weakened the family not only by assuming the role of surrogate parent and husband, but also by inculcating a moral relativism in the public schools, so that children increasingly accept out-of-wedlock childbearing, divorce, and nontraditional households as normal.

In response McLanahan remarked that it is no accident that welfare mothers face a disincentive to work. After all, when legislators created Aid to Families with Dependent Children (AFDC) — the primary welfare program for mother-only families — the program was designed to allow mothers *not* to work so they could stay home to care for their own children. People now express concern that welfare discourages work only because of the dramatic rise since the 1960's in employment among married women. On the question of why illegitimacy has risen, McLanahan felt Vedder had overemphasized the importance of welfare benefits. Looking at trends between 1955 and 1975 when AFDC benefits began declining, she could trace no more than 10-15% of the total increase in single-parent households to the increased availability and generosity of welfare benefits. Perhaps among the lowest-income population, welfare benefits may account for as much as 30 percent of the increase in mother-only families. But since illegitimacy has been rising in all income groups, McLanahan thought it a mistake to focus on the welfare system instead of looking for a theory which can explain the overall prevalence of the trend.

When Besharov asked for clarification of the differences separating the children of divorce from children born out of wedlock, McLanahan explained that most studies lump fatherless children together without distinguishing the causes of their fatherlessness. In those few studies in which researchers have compared the children of divorce with the children born out of wedlock, they have not found very big differences in their social behaviors — even though their economic situations are quite different. In economic terms, researchers see a clear hierarchy of children in mother-only families — with children of widows on top, children of divorcees coming next, and children of never-married mothers on the bottom. Countering Vedder's earlier comments, McLanahan protested that she had not proposed an improved welfare program to improve the lives of mother-only families. Rather, she saw the need for some *non*-welfare system to assist such families in ways that would not discourage work.

Vedder was intrigued by another question: Might it be possible to restore family life to what it was in 1960 by adopting different policies? Commentators now often say that such a return to the family patterns of the past is impossible, but as an economic historian, Vedder saw ample evidence that in long-term trends things often go back to the way they were 50 or 100 years ago. For instance, almost no one in 1960 would have believed that in 30 years the United States would be the largest debtor nation in the world. Since Vedder believed that the aggregate divorce rate could largely be explained with a statistical formula that includes labor-force participation rates for women, inflation rates, and welfare benefits (including housing subsidies and medical benefits), he believed that changes in government policy might actually make a big difference for family life. He noted that whereas the traditional family is now regarded as almost nonexistent among blacks, that was not the case in 1960. Vedder shared the amazement of a colleague who marvelled that while it had survived slavery, Reconstruction, and Jim Crow laws, the black family had been destroyed by the Great Society program of welfare benefits.

Unsettled by talk of relative costs of divorce and the advantages of marriage, Christensen identified memory and calculation as two contrasting — probably antithetical — principles upon which personal life might be based. Everyone understands what is meant when we say someone has a "calculating personality." Calculation kills memory, Christensen suggested, arguing that it is utterly futile to devise ways to convince people they ought to marry on the basis of calculation. Although he conceded that people do respond to incentives and although he favored making divorce more difficult, still Christensen thought the fundamental cultural problem causing the retreat from marriage is that of intergenerational amnesia, causing contemporary Americans to lose any sense of their lives as a reproduction of the patterns lived out by their grandparents. He called to mind the closing words of the Old Testament, spoken by the prophet Malachi, who anticipates a time when the Lord will turn the hearts of the fathers to the children and the hearts of the children to the fathers, warning that if the generations were not united, the whole earth would be smitten with a curse. (See Mal. 4:5, 6.) Christensen feared that if people were so far gone in living by calculation rather than memory that marriage must now be advocated as some new-fangled arrangement offering such-and-such advantages, then no ingenuity in tinkering with public policy will do any good.

In agreement with the substance of Christensen's remarks, Jones nonetheless noted that law and public policy do serve a teaching function, so shaping social attitudes. For instance, the remarkable decline in smoking in the United States can probably be traced to the Surgeon General's report on the effects of smoking and to subsequent public policies restricting the practice. Likewise, Jones believed that race relations have changed substantially in the United States not simply as a result of individual decisions, but in large part because of the passage of Civil Rights legislation in 1964.

Returning to McLanahan's paper, Besharov drew attention to the differences in the economic circumstances of white mother-only families contrasted with those of black mother-only families. Most white women in mother-only families have seen their standard of living plummet as a consequence of divorce. On the other hand, most black women in mother-only families have never married, so their economic situation has not been affected by family dissolution. These black women have not lost economic ground by having babies out of wedlock because they had no economic ground to lose.

Vedder went so far as to argue that in some cases — for poor whites as well as poor blacks — young girls may actually find some material advantage and an opportunity to achieve independence from their families by bearing a child out of wedlock and then collecting AFDC benefits.

But for Nock the primary question in investigating out-of-wedlock births was not why the mother chose to bear the child, but why she did *not* choose to marry. Unmarried young women may bear children for the same reasons as married women, but why don't they choose to marry?

In answer, Nicholi reported that adolescent mothers, particularly blacks, will tell anyone who asks that they have babies for the emotional benefits. They want someone they can love, someone who will fully love them back. These teen mothers do not bear children because of ignorance about sexuality and contraception, nor do they bear them in order to secure welfare benefits. But they typically do not marry because the young men with whom they have intercourse — especially the young black men — are totally unprepared for a family.

Donohue endorsed Nicholi's assessment of the motives of young unwed mothers. He further noted that in some neighborhoods, unwed motherhood is not only accepted, but actually constitutes a rite of passage. Among the middle-class, Donohue detected much more hypocrisy. Mother may tell her teenage daughters not to have sex before marriage, but the daughter may well scoff at such admonitions if Mom has had *The Joy of Sex* sitting on the coffee table for years and if Mom's boyfriend shows up at breakfast on Saturday mornings. When mixed messages are sent concerning a pleasurable activity, it is easy to predict which of the two messages will find acceptance.

Taking another look at the effects of the welfare system on illegitimacy, Chapman argued — against McLanahan's logic — that it simply does not matter much whether AFDC benefits have been rising or falling since 1975. It is very natural for a teenage girl to desire a baby, he reasoned. The question is one of constraints, including economic constraints, on her desire. Chapman asserted (acknowledging his debt to Charles Murray) that as long as the welfare system supplies the bare minimum needed for a young girl to establish an independent household with a baby, then the level of benefits is largely irrelevant. Even if welfare does not make the life of a single mother financially attractive, AFDC may foster illegitimacy simply by making her life economically possible.

For Gecas, out-of-wedlock births among young blacks could be explained by noting the relative scarcity of employed black men — a scarcity that has grown worse in the ghettos. Citing work in Chicago by William Julius Wilson, Gecas concluded that even if these young black women wanted a traditional nuclear family, the shortage of employed black men would make it difficult to achieve that goal.

Sampson joined in with a second endorsement of Wilson's thesis, confident that unemployment among black men was much more important than welfare benefits as a cause of black illegitimacy.

Unconvinced by Wilson's thesis, Christensen cited a recent critique of Wilson's work by Christopher Jencks, who concludes that black illegitimacy reflects cultural trends more than it does economic pressures. Popular culture has sent the message, and young blacks have received it, that marriage is not that important.

Hirschi warned against judging behaviors only by their consequences. Young women have babies out of wedlock because they have sex out of wedlock — and sex is probably all they were interested in at the time. The evidence, Hirschi noted, is fairly clear: premarital sexual activity is a species of delinquency. That is, premarital sexual activity has exactly the same causes and correlates as do other delinquent acts — robbing banks or taking illegal drugs. It therefore makes about as much sense to explain out-of-wedlock babies as the consequence of what young women want as it does to explain robbery by saying robbers want five-year prison terms. In most cases, he concluded (against Nicholi's protests), an out-of-wedlock baby is simply the unintended consequence of a bad short-term projection.

Since subsidized day care had been proposed as a way to help mother-only families, J. Craig Peery thought it necessary to caution against the risks of day care. A child in day care is a child at risk, he remarked. Good day care simply means better risk management than bad day care — but all day care represents a risk. On the matter of poverty among mother-only families, J. Craig Peery doubted whether children experienced poverty with any of the anguish adults might feel. Just as children usually do not anticipate divorce no matter how their parents fight, they do not have an alternate view of their material life, no matter how poor their family. Poverty is relative, Peery pointed out, recalling that his own grandparents lived in dirt-floored cabins, ate bulbs, and otherwise lived in ways we cannot even understand. But poverty today in America means hot and cold running water and a color television. In any case, the term *poverty* does not mean a great deal to children. Children may have no meaningful pattern at all for their lives, though, if they are raised by a single parent who regularly leaves them in a day-care center. Such children are likely to grow up desperately void of loving relationships, yet willing to seek such a relationship by themselves having a baby out of wedlock — just like their mothers. Once such a pattern is set, it may be impossible to stop it from self-perpetuating.

With Chapman, Carlson thought Charles Murray's work deserved attention. In the conclusion of *Losing Ground*, Murray proposes as a thought experiment the abolition of all welfare benefits from government altogether. What would happen? In Carlson's version of this thought experiment, people would not starve because they would reorganize themselves into something we would call families. Carlson believed that in the absence of government intervention, broadly defined, families still make basic economic sense. The family defines the place where people share and cooperate for economic gains. The family also permits expression of the most basic human sentiments, including the need for companionship, the urge to procreate, the desire for security. The family is the kind of social unit that someone who could invent would invent, because it meets so many basic needs.

Returning to the mundane world of history, Carlson noted that when Congress first created AFDC, the initial intent was that of providing for widows and for abandoned married women. Provision for never-married mothers came later and even then such provision was still considered to be a minor addition to a program principally designed to help women who had been married. But over time, the proportion of AFDC benefits going to unwed mothers grew. Now unwed mothers are the principal beneficiaries of the program. This shift in AFDC beneficiaries simply does not reflect the intent of those who established the program, raising serious questions in Carlson's mind about the proper way to construct public policy.

Detecting a persistent concern among participants about values and morals, Besharov recalled how Ingrid Bergman was once driven out of the country for bearing a child out of wedlock. In contrast, at the most recent Academy Awards, at least four cohabiting couples with babies appeared as models of glamour and sexuality.

Gardner interpreted the visibility of cohabiting parents in film stardom as evidence of a double standard: the child of unmarried parents in Hollywood is a "love child"; the child of unmarried parents in the ghetto is "illegitimate." Cultural and governmental leaders need to do a better job of encouraging marriage, Gardner asserted. For example, the Chicago Housing Authority recently informed tenants of a project that those who were not married or related to someone on a lease would have to leave. As a consequence, eight previously cohabiting couples were married in a mass ceremony, with gowns, tuxedos, hairdressing services, limos, and honeymoon hotel rooms all donated by local businesses. Six months later [as of shortly before the conference], all eight married couples were still together; seven of the eight husbands were employed.

In Nock's mind, the mass wedding in Chicago might mean that marriage is best promoted through greater reliance upon local institutions — such as churches, schools, neighborhoods — where people still know others involved and actions are not anonymous. Nock thought it unfortunate that Americans now tend not to look to local institutions, "mediating structures" in Peter Berger's phrase, when seeking solutions to social problems.

But perhaps people don't trust local institutions, Besharov countered, because such institutions have failed them.

But local institutions have failed largely because they have been weakened by government intervention, Jones protested. Why now if a Quaker is shunned, he can go to court for a court order compelling other Quakers to stop shunning him!

When Besharov complained that in his Unitarian Church he never heard anything supporting marriage and family, Carlson joined in a broader indictment of mainline Protestant churches, which have generally moved to the social gospel and abandoned the questions of personal morality essential to family life. One of the problems of relying on "mediating institutions" such as churches, volunteer organizations, or charities is that most are simply another kind of bureaucracy, in Carlson's estimation.

To make the case that current family woes are cultural not economic, Donohue contrasted the two decades of the 20th century — the 1930's and the 1960's — when welfare benefits grew dramatically, but with different effects on the character of the recipients. In the 1930's, the Depression years, people received public assistance for purely economic reasons. But in the 1960's, the explosion in welfare benefits took place when the unemployment rate stood at 4 percent. In other words, the dramatic growth in welfare benefits was not a response to economic need. Rather, Donohue believed that welfare benefits rose at the time because of the emerging ethic of entitlement. He could recall activists in the 1960's urging that everyone — especially blacks — who was even marginally eligible be added to the welfare rolls so that the cities would be bankrupted, forcing the federal government to adopt socialism.

Wilson's explanation of black illegitimacy failed for Donohue because it focuses only on the unemployment of black men, not on their labor-force participation rates. Until the late 1960's, the labor-force participation rate among blacks ran as high or higher than among whites. But since then, the labor-force participation rate has declined, especially for blacks. Besides, Donohue contended, if unemployment is causing the breakdown of the black family, then why are Asian immigrants succeeding economically in urban areas? Young Asian teenagers are quite willing to take minimum-wage jobs working for "chump change" even though many young black males refuse such employment. The young Asians realize that hard work at low-paying jobs can lead to better things in the future.

McLanahan accused Donohue of giving an inaccurate picture of unemployment among black males. She noted that unemployment among black males rose steadily from 1955 on — except for a sharp drop about the time of the Vietnam War. Among young black males, the steady rise in unemployment was even more remarkable. While she conceded that economic trends cannot fully explain what has happened to black families, she faulted Donohue for his willingness to dismiss unemployment among black males as unimportant. Perhaps after 20 years of bleak employment prospects, many blacks have succumbed to a hopelessness that is now part of their culture, McLanahan suggested. New Asian immigrants are still buoyed up by hope that motivates them economically. Besides, Asians are winning their success entrepreneurially, as the Jews did at the turn of the century, by turning some initial capital into sales opportunities. Blacks, who have never had any sort of capital, moved into jobs as janitors and maids when they made their migration into the cities.

As an economic historian who studies labor-force statistics, Vedder tried to adjudicate the dispute between Donohue and McLanahan. He agreed with McLanahan that black unemployment has risen over time, has risen dramatically, and has risen relative to unemployment among whites. Today the unemployment rate among blacks runs two-and-one-half times higher than the rate among whites, with an even wider gap separating young blacks from young whites. But Vedder was intrigued by a long-term trend evident in a different statistic, namely the employment ratio, defined as the number employed divided by the number of adults in the population. In 1955, the employment ratio among blacks was *higher* than that among whites (approximately 59 percent vs. 56 percent). Today, however, the white employment ratio stands significantly higher than the black employment ratio (approximately 64 percent vs. 57 percent). Why has this happened? Vedder conjectured that over time changes in public policy, especially welfare policy, have affected blacks more than whites, while changes in the market economy have influenced whites more than blacks.

Regardless of what caused current levels of unemployment among blacks, Chapman agreed with Wilson about the harmful effects of such unemployment on young blacks, who often grow up in communities where they know no one who holds down a steady job. Chapman judged it almost impossible to devise a public policy that would guide young people raised in such circumstances toward long-term, economically productive activity.

Biting his finger a bit with nervousness, Besharov broached the subject — considered out of bounds by many commentators — of how, in shifting the ground rules for labor-force participation, government may have helped white women gain employment in ways that have hurt black men. Orthodox economists still maintain that more jobs for women simply create more employment for everyone, Besharov noted, but a growing number of analysts dissent from this view, arguing that at least during the last 20 years black men have had to compete with women — predominantly white women — for jobs.

This alleged discrimination in favor of white women over black men reminded Carlson of a deliberate move by policymakers in Sweden trying to curb an influx of immigrant workers from Turkey, the Balkans, and elsewhere. Because this influx was causing social strains, Swedish policymakers explicitly decided to adopt measures to move more Swedish women into the workforce rather than try to make up the labor-force shortage by employing hard-to-assimilate immigrants. Carlson gave credence to reports that American employers, operating on a similar logic, prefer a middle-class white woman over a lower-class black male. But because such employment preferences raise such difficult questions, they are rarely investigated.

Vedder sought to explain racial disparities in employment as the predictable consequences of two different types of public policy. On the one hand, government leaders have helped middle-class and upper-middle class citizens move into employment through the adoption of child-care tax credits and other measures. In Vedder's view, such "yuppie public policies" had succeeded too well, pushing white labor-force participation so high that it has weakened marriage and family life. On the other hand, the government has adopted policies for the low-income population—disproportionately black — that have discouraged employment.

Reverting to the question about day care, Jones deplored the trend in current debates towards a rigorously irreligious policy governing proposed benefits for child care. More broadly, Jones perceived a pervasive bias in public policy against religious institutions. For instance, when the Salvation Army conducts drug and alcohol rehabilitation clinics in public housing in New York, government officials forbid the Army from doing what it usually does, that is, inviting people to come to Jesus and give up the demon rum and syringe and be saved.

Depressed by the drift of the conversation, Peery conceded that Americans need to look to public policy as a teacher, but he argued that it is going to be a dismal teacher in any case. The real transmitters of values about family life, about right and wrong, will be the parents. The success of marriage and family life depends heavily on expectations that are partly conveyed by government policy, but more decisively shaped by individual parents. Peery believed that in general Asians and blacks are separated by a profound difference in mental outlook: Asians think they have some control over their lives; blacks do not. This difference in outlook comes from family life, not government policy.

But to illustrate how government action can make a difference in family life, Anderson cited a case recently before the Supreme Court, *Michael H. and Victoria D.* v. *Gerald D.* The case asked the justices to decide if a man can make a legal claim of paternity to a child born to a married couple living together. Such claims are forbidden under one of the most fundamental rules of common law regarding marriage, but in a 5-4 decision the Supreme Court only narrowly upheld California's prohibition of such claims. The four justices in dissent argued that in our democratic, pluralistic society, it is perverse to give legal priority to families based on marriage. Even the judges in the majority seemed to believe that the law they upheld was merely a permissible policy prerogative, not a fundamental premise of marriage law. Anderson believed that in this and other rulings the Supreme Court had so blurred the legal distinction between marriage and singleness that a marriage license now means very little in American society. He feared that as long as legal marriage means so little, it will remain quite difficult to convince unmarried couples that they ought to marry.

Nock perceived surrogate motherhood as a different sort of threat to the legal foundations of marriage. Under traditional assumptions of law, a child born to a married woman would belong to her and her husband. However, when a married woman consents to become a surrogate mother for another couple, the contract assigns parenthood of the child to the biological father. Surrogacy — a dreadful practice in Nock's view — requires fundamental alteration of a whole host of family laws. Just as contraception separated sex from procreation, surrogacy is now separating biology from parenthood in a strange way.

Nicholi traced the contemporary ills of family life to an enormous change of values over the past 40 or 50 years, as society has abandoned moral and spiritual values in favor of material ones. The family isn't valued much in this new moral context. Yet Nicholi was amazed at the universal preoccupation with ethics and morality, manifest in Washington, on Wall Street, and within the universities. This preoccupation does not mean Americans have suddenly become very moral and ethical in reaction to the nation's cultural drift. Rather, Nicholi interpreted the preoccupation with ethics and morality as a result of confusion on the issue. How do we get out of this situation? he asked.

Proffering no answer to that question, Carlson nonetheless ventured to identify one other possible cause of family dissolution. Industrial capitalism, as Karl Marx pointed out, tends to divide traditional communities and families into individuals whose abilities can be most efficiently allocated if they are not tied down by tradition or by devotion to any specific locality. While families are in one sense economically viable and beneficial, capitalists tend to see them as inefficient remnants of socialism operating by the dictum "From each according to his ability, to each according to his need." Carlson turned to Vedder, asking him as an economic historian to explain to what degree capitalism might be held responsible for the decay of family life.

In Vedder's view, the family has suffered from the pervasive cultural movement toward materialism, a movement broader than capitalism *per se*. Vedder noted that in premodern times, most children (who survived) spent almost all their time with their parents. Even in the early decades of the Industrial Revolution, children went into the factories with their parents. Only in the 19th and 20th centuries have children been frequently separated from their parents. This separation of parents from children was caused partly by parents' employment someplace other than at home or on the farm. But parents were separated from children in part because as incomes rose so did aspirations, requiring the establishment of schools for children. In modern times, the separation of parents from children has grown even more pronounced, as more wives go to work and as children spend more time in day care, little league, and summer camps. Yet since the separation of parent and child is not as severe in the capitalist states as in the Communist Soviet Union where the state is antifamily (for various political reasons), Vedder thought it a mistake to indict capitalism *per se* for the modern erosion of family life. Economic development itself in modern materialistic civilization — capitalist and noncapitalist — has separated parents from children.

Elaborating on Nicholi's comment about the current preoccupation with ethics, Christensen argued that constant fretting about moral rules does not happen for a person or society informed by a strong sense of moral purpose. Only when we lack a guiding and animating sense of moral purpose do we fumble around and agonize constantly over rules of ethics. Picking up the economic theme pursued by Vedder and Carlson, Christensen identified economic efficiency as a goal in tension with the pursuit of moral excellence. Borrowing from the work of Alasdair MacIntyre, Christensen said that some activities which cultivate moral excellence are economically very inefficient. For instance, it is economically inefficient for mothers to stay home to care for their own children, yet doing so fosters moral excellence. But when pursuit of economic benefit displaces the cultivation of morality, society may discover that the sought-for gain in efficiency does not last because people have been demoralized by being reduced to bits of a machine, moral ciphers. Inspiring moral commitment proves especially difficult as society grows more secular in the ways Jones had mentioned. Christensen recalled the late Victorian complaint of John Ruskin, who confessed perplexity in *The Crown of Wild Olive* about how to appeal to an audience consisting of both believers and unbelievers. Some moral appeals may win assent from those who believe in a life hereafter and in divine judgment, yet may carry little force among those who believe that if they do not satisfy their desires here and now, there is nothing else.

When Nicholi asked how to resolve this dilemma, Christensen answered that it must be worked out heart by heart, soul by soul, not by an act of Congress. This response did not satisfy Nicholi, who perceived a national confusion on moral questions. This confusion not only pervades our major political, economic, and educational institutions, it also strongly affects family life. Christensen agreed that moral confusion does indeed affect family life, recalling his own investigation of the apparent correlation between the sharp drop in Catholic fertility and the simultaneous decline in memorial masses for the dead. People who do not care about their ancestors do not care about their posterity.

Sounding a hopeful note, Peery pointed out (at the risk of sounding self-congratulatory) that all present had lived through the cultural shifts being discussed, yet all remained committed to family life. Determining how that happened would help others do the same, he concluded.

Rather than address Peery's question, Donohue ventured a partial explanation of the moral uncertainty so troubling to Nicholi. The emergence of an "inverse utilitarianism" (defined as "the greatest good for the least number of people") has made it almost impossible to establish a moral consensus. In part because of actions taken by the American Civil Liberties Union, civil liberty now often takes priority over custom, tradition, or social convention. The "rights binge" is not over, Donohue remarked. Intoxicated with rights, many Americans have lost interest in traditional concomitant responsibilities. Nor is the market economy necessarily to blame. A century ago in the 1880's, when this country witnessed the heyday of laissez-faire capitalism — before the Sherman antitrust legislation, yet after slavery — the country did not have the kind of family dissolution evident today. Nor does family life appear weak in Japan, another capitalist country. However, Japanese employers and employees do operate under a different conception of inclusion, so that a person employed by Sony at age 18 will probably still be there at age 68. Donohue interpreted both the greed on Wall Street today and the sleaze in government as symptomatic of a general promiscuity. Promiscuity for some people means indulgence in drugs, for others it means sex, for others it is money — but an eroded sense of restraint is manifest in all forms of promiscuity.

Such talk struck Hirschi as too gloomy. He saw evidence that social trends may have turned around. He recalled his years at Berkeley in the 1960's when at many weddings the bride was holding a child. But that is not what he had seen lately (most immediately in his own daughters' marriages). More broadly,

Hirschi noted that drug use was down and that crime has also peaked and may be in a down cycle. Divorce has leveled off. Since most social problems run in parallel cycles, Americans may hope for improvements on other fronts as well. In Hirschi's opinion, many people have lived through the consequences of past behaviors, have been punished for twenty years of lack of restraint, and are modifying their behavior accordingly.

Not as positive in his outlook, Anderson believed that current family woes stem in part from a deep ambiguity about what it means to be a father today. Defined by biology and by the demands of nurturing, motherhood carries a clear meaning; but fatherhood is less well defined than in the past. Anderson blamed American policymakers for institutionalizing a kind of antifamilism that has affected men more than women.

Repeating Peery's remark that all present had somehow retained a commitment to family life despite the cultural turbulence of recent decades, Jones believed that conference participants were not as unrepresentative of the nation as a whole as might be supposed. His experience in living in various neighborhoods suggested that most Americans still share a moral consensus about family life, but that they feel intimidated by a highly visible minority. Perhaps because America is a media-driven society, Americans let an unrepresentative minority set the agenda for public discussion, so skewing conclusions about prevailing social attitudes. Inclined to agree with Hirschi that Americans are behaving more soberly than in the past, Jones felt that average Americans needed to reassess the validity of their values, without feeling defensive in doing so.

Turning to a narrower question, Carlson asked McLanahan to explain why her research appeared to show that remarriage of a divorced spouse does not improve social outcomes for children.

McLanahan responded by noting the relative ineffectiveness of stepfathers in disciplining stepchildren, especially stepdaughters. When a grandmother moves into a single-parent household, the family begins to behave more like a two-parent household — but when a stepparent moves in, the consequences are not so favorable for children. If the grandmother comes into the single-parent household, she is probably helping the children, whereas a stepfather may actually be competing with the children for the mother's time. Some research suggests that mothers in stepparent families spend less time with their children than do mothers in intact first marriages. A stepfather usually spends considerably less time with the children than does a natural father. McLanahan was uncertain whether the typical stepfather felt less attached to the children than do natural fathers or whether the children rejected him. In any case, the generally negative outcome seen among stepchildren makes it hard to believe that the problems in single-parent households are principally caused by depressed income. Stepfamilies enjoy an average income closer to the income of two-parent households (even when the stepfather pays child support to a previous wife) than single-parent households, yet stepfamilies still seem to foster the same adverse outcomes for children. McLanahan reported some preliminary data suggesting that living in a stepfamily causes problems chiefly for the oldest sibling, a pattern that would lend credence to the idea that the stepparent competes with the oldest child for position in the family.

Proposing an alternative explanation of what happens in stepfamilies, Peery conjectured that divorce may often be a symptom of a parental deficiency not remedied by remarriage. Until that deficiency is corrected, it will continue to cause problems for the children.

For Nock, the problem in stepfamilies was the lack of generational boundaries, which disappear once there is only one parent (usually the mother) and her child, who become like peers. Generational boundaries are not reestablished by remarriage, at least not for the stepparent. In contrast, a grandmother coming into the home can discipline because a generational boundary still exists between her and the children.

The ambiguities surrounding stepfatherhood are only an intensification of the ambiguities surrounding fatherhood itself, Gecas observed. More broadly, the dissolution of family life does not reflect deliberate decisions so much as it does unintended consequences of actions in law, in the economy, and in welfare policy. Cumulatively, these unintended consequences have made it increasingly tough to maintain a stable family. Modern society — a society of industry, bureaucracy, and mass culture — caters to the individual, not to the family as a unit. Divorce is no mystery; family dissolution is no puzzle. Rather than ask what is causing the family to break down, perhaps it makes more sense to ask, What features of contemporary American society encourage stability and continuity in the family? The list of answers to that question, Gecas remarked, would run much shorter than would a list of social forces contributing to the instability of the family.

Hirschi opened the third session of the conference by summarizing his paper on crime and the family. He underscored the strong correlation between crime and family functioning as manifest in parental supervision, discipline, and affection. Researchers have identified a statistical correlation between crime and family structure, but this correlation is not strong, suggesting that the broken home is not a good place to begin discussion of the connection between family life and crime. Hirschi complained that academic disciplines too often start with their favorite causes rather than with the phenomenon requiring explanation. To reverse that tendency in the current instance meant looking at crime itself. What is crime? Crime is attempting to get something for nothing: money without work, sex without courtship, exhilaration without accomplishment. However crimes may differ, all are quick, easy ways to pleasure unrestrained by concern for long-term consequences or costs. But crimes universally entail long-term costs, Hirschi noted, including injury, death, and disease. These natural consequences may be more important than the law as sanctions against crime. Many behaviors not legally defined as crime share essentially the same character, including truancy (from school, from home, from marriage) and quitting (school, job, marriage). All of these types of truancy and quitting produce immediate benefits while imposing long-term costs — so do murder, suicide, rape, reckless driving, smoking, and shoplifting. Indeed, researchers find a reasonably clear statistical correlation between all of these types of behavior, including those not legally defined as crime. Offenders do not specialize, progress, or change in their career, although criminal acts do decline in frequency after middle adolescence or early adulthood. Consistent with the theory that crime is an attempt to get something for nothing, offenders are not very persistent, but are easily deterred.

With evident relish, Hirschi skewered several popular but faulty explanations of crime. Psychiatry sees offenders as driven to crime by forces over which they have little control, but why then are offenders so easily deterred? Economic theory sees crime as an alternative to labor-force participation, when in fact crime (as non-

or anti-economic activity) is the opposite of work. The notion of "organized crime" dissolves under scrutiny, since it is impossible to construct a viable social organization out of individuals all trying to get something for nothing. Hirschi identified his own theory of crime as one rooted in the venerable theory of social- or self-control. This theory assumes that everyone likes to have fun, everyone likes to avoid irritation, so we must all be trained to waive or delay or control our impulses. Where does this training occur? Typically, this training occurs in the family early in life. Those who have not learned self-control will have difficulty accepting the restraints of employment, education, and marriage. Predictably, not only is lack of restraint often traceable to past failures in family life, but such a lack will itself cause future disorder in homelife as well.

In conclusion, Hirschi announced a finding not included in the original version of his paper: namely, that the size of the family is consistently related to delinquency among children. The effects upon delinquency of the number of siblings indeed appear stronger than do the effects of household structure. Interpreting this provocative finding in light of his own theory of crime, Hirschi speculated that the size of a family predicts deviant behavior in the children because it is itself an indicator of parental self-control or its absence. Hirschi hastened to add that no one would suggest that bearing children within marriage is itself deviant behavior; yet, he asserted that behavior motivationally analogous to crime is fairly often involved in the process. No one should be surprised, then, if undisciplined behavior by parents portends theoretically equivalent behavior in their children. This hypothesis entails a reasonably direct policy implication: Americans should worry less about strengthening the family to prevent crime and should focus more on training people in self-control to strengthen the family.

Discussant for Hirschi's paper, Sampson expressed agreement with its major arguments. He noted that historically sociologists have explained crime as acts committed out of economic need or relative deprivation. The influence of family life on crime received little attention because of this theoretical bias. Sampson praised Hirschi's work on delinquency in the late 1960's as revolutionary in its focus on social control, especially as exercised by the family. Not only did Hirschi's theory break with past assumptions about the nature of crime, but it actually succeeded in explaining patterns of delinquency. Previously unacquainted with Hirschi's new finding that family size predicts delinquency, however, Sampson withheld judgment on that particular issue, pending further investigation.

Although in agreement with Hirschi that family function influences crime more than family structure does, Sampson still thought Hirschi had understated the importance of family structure in his paper. The research does indeed show a relatively small simple or direct relationship between family structure and crime. But family structure can *indirectly* affect delinquency through its influence upon parent-child attachment and upon parental supervision. Sampson reported that in his own work, he had found weaker social controls — and therefore more delinquency — in homes disrupted either through divorce or separation. Further, family disruption can indirectly affect crime through its effects upon the broader community. That is, family disruption affects not only the children of the separating parents, but other children in the neighborhood also. In areas where most households are two-parent families, parents supervise not only their own children, but neighbors' children as well. In contrast, in areas where female-headed households predominate, few social controls restrain the activities of teenagers. This does not mean that in such areas the children from broken homes commit all the crimes. What it does mean is that a high incidence of family disruption will drive up the crime rate in the community, regardless of its composition by race, age, or social class. Though uncertain about the relationship posited by Hirschi between family size and delinquency, Sampson expressed confidence that its validity could be empirically tested.

In response to Sampson's critique of his paper, Hirschi agreed that the effects of family structure upon community and neighborhood deserved consideration, since such effects might be more important than those discussed in the paper. Asked about the size of the effects he was seeing for family structure and for family size, Hirschi replied first that the rate of delinquency in the broken home ran about 30 percent higher than in intact homes, second that the percentage of teens with a police record rose steadily from 14 percent among teens with no siblings to 43 percent among teens from families with five or more children. Hirschi compared the relationship between delinquency and family size to the relationship between academic achievement and family size.

Why, then, Christensen asked, did researchers find that among Mormon (Latter-day Saint) households in New Mexico and Utah, premarital sexual activity — essentially criminal in nature, by Hirschi's theory — was more common among adolescents from small families than among peers from large families?

Hirschi was skeptical about the reported finding, but he conceded the possibility that perhaps when large families reflect religious values, then the parents' motivation will come from long-term commitments, not the short-term impulses characteristic of crime.

Against Hirschi's claim that academic achievement falls as family size grows, Peery cited work by Richard Galbraith and Sandra Scarr attacking the "dumber by the dozen" theory of child psychology as invalid.

Offering a personal response to Hirschi's posited relationship between large families and delinquency, Anderson recalled seeing two quite different types of large families as he grew up. On the one hand, he could remember large families in which every one of the children was involved in some sort of delinquent behavior. Yet on the other hand, he had also seen other families, just as large, in which the parents had reared a large family because of religious motivation and in which the children were more successful and exemplary than children from smaller families. Anderson felt a need to make some distinction between these two types of families lest Hirschi's results be used in some way to disparage religiously motivated parents with large families. Parents who for religious reasons bear a large number of children may actually be exercising greater self-control than parents with few children, especially if the parents with large families control their childbearing through abstinence while the parents of small families control their fertility in a different fashion.

Reinterpreting Hirschi's finding, McLanahan reasoned that large families may foster delinquency not because parents lack self-control, but because the larger the number of children the less parent there is to go around to provide supervision. A large number of children reduces the ratio of parents to children in the family, just as the absence of a parent does. McLanahan felt the issue raised by Anderson might be addressed differently by determining the relationships between family size and children's behavior — delinquency, academic achievement, success — *within* religious groups that promote large families. She supposed that it could still be the case that within such groups, children from large families do not do well.

Hirschi could not see evidence supporting McLanahan's conjecture that lack of parental supervision explained delinquency in large families, since the relationship between family size and delinquency persisted even if older children had moved out of the house.

Although Nicholi felt certain that the number of children would affect the accessibility of parents to their children, he regarded family size as merely one of many variables affecting the availability of parents to their children. The relegation of care for children to agencies outside the home has weakened parent-child ties, as has the intrusion of the television set into the home. In almost any American home now, interaction occurs between the electronic box and the figures sitting around in the dark, rather than between parents and their children.

With Anderson, Nicholi felt that when parents rear many children for religious reasons, large family size may reflect self-control, not lack of self-control. Hirschi conceded that this question needed investigation, perhaps by looking at large Mormon or Catholic families.

Hirschi's characterization of crime as an uncontrolled impulse brought to Nicholi's mind a shift in the last twenty years in the reasons people see psychiatrists. In the past, people consulted psychiatrists because of inability to express feelings and impulses. Now, however, people come to psychiatrists because of inability to control impulses. Nicholi cited psychiatric studies that trace lack of discipline to an absence of a father in the home. Researchers have noted unusual behavior problems, traceable to lack of internal control, among children of fathers who spent long periods of time away from home, such as Norwegian sailors and American military men.

If large families foster delinquency, Vedder wondered, why then have crime rates climbed at the same time that average family size has dropped? Does that mean that if family size had *not* declined, crime rates in the 1960's and 1970's would have risen even more dramatically?

Confessing a personal bias against Hirschi's finding, Carlson nonetheless acknowledged its historical plausibility. Juvenile de-

linquency first became a matter of widespread public concern in the
1830's and 1840's — concern which led to the reform-school movement — at a time of high birth rates. Public concern over juvenile
delinquency again became visible at the turn of the century, when
juvenile justice systems were first established, at a time of heavy
immigration as many very large families from southern Europe
entered the United States. Once again, juvenile delinquency became
a headline issue in the 1950's and 1960's during the baby boom.
Carlson concluded by asking Hirschi if there were not some opti-
mum number of children — say, perhaps two or three — that
parents could rear without losing some of the control they would
have with only one child.

When Hirschi replied that all measures of delinquency rise
steadily from one-child families right on up, Vedder joked that the
optimal family size is zero children, and Nock chimed in that
without any juveniles, juvenile delinquency would surely disappear.

Donohue reiterated Vedder's point that families have declined in
size, yet crime rates have not. Except for the Irish, who have had
a high crime rate, Donohue argued that large Catholic families
have not fostered crime in the past.

Citing his own previous article entitled "Hellfire and Delinquency," Hirschi noted that religiosity does not appear to affect criminality — except for drug use. But Nicholi doubted whether a
conventional look at religiosity would suffice. He recalled work by
one of his graduate students who had investigated conversion
experiences among undergraduates. Internal religious experience
seemed to affect drug use, heavy drinking, and other behaviors
more profoundly than did mere church attendance.

McLanahan did not share others' puzzlement about how crime
rates could rise while families shrank. In fact, she pointed out,
crime rates surged upward just as children born during the baby
boom (between 1947 and 1957) started to enter adolescence in the
1960's. Demographic patterns are quite consistent with Hirschi's
views, she concluded.

Gecas persisted in the belief that parental supervision is more
important than parental self-control for explaining juvenile delinquency. Further, he asked, had Hirschi investigated the effects on
delinquency of supervision by grandparents, uncles, aunts, and
other adults in the family?

Hirschi protested that his evidence simply did not support the belief that parental supervision explains the relationship between family size and delinquency. Supervision by extended family does have some effect, but not nearly as large as that he had found linked to family size.

Government statistics, Christensen noted, show that less than half of all men in prison and less than 30 percent of adolescents in state institutions have been reared by two biological parents. Whereas Hirschi had reported that criminal activity in general decreases with age, could it not be — Christensen conjectured — that adolescents from intact families are much more likely than adolescents from broken homes to "wise up" after committing one or two delinquent acts?

Delinquents do indeed penetrate the criminal justice system further if they do not have strong parents behind them than if they do, Hirschi acknowledged, so that the further one moves into the criminal justice system the more likely one is to find offenders from broken families.

Still unsettled by the notion that parents rear large families because of a lack of personal self-control, Anderson reminded conference participants that traditionally Christianity defined procreation as the fundamental purpose of marriage, while identifying companionship of spouses as a secondary purpose. It is true that since Vatican II the Catholic Church has largely stopped making the primary-secondary distinction, so equating procreation and spousal companionship, but procreation remains a central purpose of marriage in Christian thought. From a theological perspective, couples marry not merely to procreate but to care for, nurture, rear, and educate children. Anderson explained that the Catholic doctrine of the indissolubility of marriage makes sense because of the long-term commitment required to rear a child. Public officials ought to keep this religious tradition in mind, Anderson concluded, in framing policies affecting marriage and family. Without wishing to quarrel with Anderson's description of traditional Christian attitudes toward family life, Hirschi doubted that motives for having large families have shifted much historically, since Sampson possessed statistics from the 1930's showing the same relationship between delinquency and family size which Hirschi had uncovered in contemporary statistics.

Returning to Sampson's earlier observations about the relationship between crime and concentration of single-parent households, Peery judged large-tract public housing for the poor as disastrously wrong-headed because such housing brings together so many female-headed households. In general, policymakers should try to keep neighborhoods smaller rather than larger and should help communities and other social networks to reinforce the kind of supervision that families give.

Sampson confirmed that the proportion of multi-unit residences in a community is a strong predictor of crime rates, regardless of the race or economic class of the community. However, in his view, large public housing projects foster crime more because of the way they concentrate population than because of the character of the households found there.

Lack of parental supervision is not a problem peculiar to dense inner-city neighborhoods, Gardner remarked. In the last decade, "the neighborhood mom" has appeared as a phenomenon in suburban neighborhoods in which only one mother will be at home during the day. Children from the entire neighborhood will identify this woman as the person elementary-school officials should call in case of emergency. Gardner interpreted this as evidence of a new anonymity in suburban culture and of a loss of social control in even the best neighborhoods.

If Americans stopped sending all of our old people to Arizona, Hirschi suggested, they could be guarding the neighborhoods back home, especially since offenders are easily deterred.

Raising a more theoretical question, Vedder sketched out a possible economic interpretation of Hirschi's definition of crime as a lack of self-control as a preference for immediate rather than deferred satisfactions. Noting the importance of time preference as an explanatory concept in economics, Vedder wondered if indulgence in debt and aversion to saving could not be regarded as economic delinquency. Perhaps the nation as a whole is now engaged in economic delinquency, he ventured. Vedder reasoned that a correlation between crime and debt probably exists, especially since young people save less than older people.

Consistent with Vedder's hypothesis, Hirschi cited data on the savings rate and the household finances of families in which delinquents are reared.

Expanding upon a topic broached by Gardner, Christensen observed that as an increasing number of wives move into paid employment, crime rates among children from intact families will probably look more like those of single-parent families, because two married parents who are both employed cannot supervise their children much more than a single unmarried parent.

Sampson agreed that crime rates — especially for property crimes — rise as adults move outside the home, whether divorce or employment is causing the movement out of the home. According to one theory, crime rose in the 1960's even though wealth in general was also going up not only because there were more goods to steal but also because there were fewer people around to guard the home by noting the presence of strangers in the neighborhood.

Stressing the importance of community ties, McLanahan identified church attendance within a community as an important measure of the strength of those ties. Amplifying this theme, Sampson noted a correlation between church attendance within a community and the crime rate. The strength or absence of cohesion in a community in some ways accounts for the difference in crime rates. Religion as such was not the deterrent of crime, in Sampson's view, but rather the controls and expectations prevailing in a community of regular churchgoers. From this perspective, controlling crime depends not so much on law enforcement by government officials as upon the informal controls exercised by families in communities.

But if unlegislated parental attitudes are so important, Chapman was hard pressed to understand how the Irish, once one of the most crime-prone groups in the nation, had become one of the least criminal ethnic groups. How does an ethnic group break out of a cycle of criminality?

Hirschi explained that in the general pattern for American immigrants, the first generation commits few crimes, but that the second generation — the children born of immigrant parents — commits a large number of crimes. Sociologists explain this as the consequence of the breakdown of family and local control, as children learn a new language in the new country and as conflict with their parents increases. High crime rates were even found among the Jews at one time. However, crime rates tend to decline over time as immigrant groups adjust to American society. When Chapman interrupted to ask how children can learn self-control from parents who did not have it, Hirschi answered that the exigencies of life tend to punish deviant behavior naturally in ways that, over time, discourage crime. The state and the family can merely impose punishment for behavior that normally incurs natural consequences. Accordingly, groups can become more conforming over time as a result of the experience of living. The law and family sanctions against deviant behaviors are simply attempts to warn people against the natural consequences of the behaviors. Blacks are the only ethnic group, however, which has not followed the American immigrant pattern of greater conformity, less crime, in later generations.

When Chapman asked him to explain in what way blacks are an exception, Hirschi replied that according to self-report surveys, young blacks do not commit many more crimes than young whites do. Black delinquents, however, make up a disproportionate fraction of youth in state institutions and in the criminal justice system. Perhaps weak black families allow their delinquent children to penetrate the criminal justice system further than do the white families of offending adolescents. In any case, Hirschi stressed that the vast majority of all races conform to social norms. The idea that everyone commits delinquent acts is simply a myth of our times.

Trying to grasp the unifying meaning of Hirschi's paper, Carlson identified two central themes: first, that family breakdown raises the level of crime to some degree; second, that "family buildup" — that is, having children — also encourages crime. Which is worse? Carlson queried. Does family breakdown do more to cause crime than family buildup?

On the basis of available data, Hirschi concluded that family buildup has the more deleterious effects in fostering crime.

Can it really be the case, Christensen asked, that criminals do not specialize in their offenses? What about the particularly grievous crimes of rape and murder? After all, rates for rape have gone up even in times when rates for other crimes have gone down. How can that be if criminals do not specialize? Aren't murder and rape acts of a hardened criminal, not merely the impulsive acts of a happy-go-lucky sort of person that Hirschi's theory seems to describe? In particular, Christensen recalled seeing research on teen murderers and violent rapists, finding a high level of family disruption in the backgrounds of these offenders.

Officially reported rates for rape, Hirschi responded, do not carry much credibility among criminologists, who generally believe that although the rate of *reported* rape has changed, the actual incidence of rape has not.

But, Sampson added, rates for rape do rise and fall with rates for burglary in a way that accords with Hirschi's hypothesis that criminals do not specialize in particular kinds of offenses. In many cases, a criminal will commit a rape if the opportunity presents itself. A criminal breaks into a house to burglarize it, but will commit a rape if there is a female with no guardian present. The Boston Strangler was caught because of a burglary, not his rapes.

Still unconvinced, Christensen persisted in the belief that some criminals must surely nurse particular grievances against the world, grievances which are well defined — not simply impulsive — and which motivate them in particular ways. Isn't it the case, for instance, that some rapists harbor a particular grudge against women and so turn to rape as a way of getting back at women?

FBI statistics for rapists, Hirschi replied, show long-term versatility in offenses — an ordinary mixture of offenses, not a singular fixation on rape. People who do have particular grievances against the world are almost by definition people capable of carrying out long-term projects which are inconsistent with crime — which is a short-term project. People who would assassinate the President, for instance, are not ordinary criminals. With good reason, the Secret Service does not consider ordinary criminals a threat to the President. There may indeed be a population of people who do grievous things because of grudges, but they are a small population unrepresentative of most criminals.

As a chilling illustration of the senseless impulsiveness of rape, McLanahan noted the "wilding" in New York City's Central Park in April 1989 in which a gang of young blacks raped, brutalized, and almost killed a white woman jogger. The teens involved did not appear to have a motive for this horrible act, but rather just seemed to be out to have a good time. Herself a resident of New York City at the time, McLanahan recalled that many citizens were particularly shocked, unable to explain how such a thing could happen since so many of these boys were in school and lived in two-parent families in apartments with doormen. According to one explanation, two-parent families can be horrible, too: if the father beats the child every night, it will make him more violent than being reared by a single mother. But another explanation (which received little attention at the time) is that in a neighborhood in which social networks are totally broken apart, controls on the teen from a two-parent household are not much different from those on a teen from a one-parent household. The social control of teenagers depends not only on what is happening in the household, but also upon what is happening in the community.

Not persuaded that crime springs from nothing but wild impulsiveness, Vedder defended an economist's view of crime, which assumes that criminals are usually rational people who try to maximize their personal satisfaction. Crime rates have risen in recent decades because crime has paid more in the 1970's and 80's than in the 50's and 60's as costs of committing crime have fallen. The benefits of crime accrue immediately, while the costs — always uncertain, since the criminal does not know if he will be caught — lie in the future. Crime makes sense to those willing to pursue short-term economic advantage and to discount possible future costs.

Hirschi acknowledged that criminologists owe a debt to the utilitarian model essential to economics. But he complained that the economic model of crime lays too much emphasis on state sanctions, which criminologists regard as too far removed to have any impact, at least within a liberal democratic society. If the state imposes draconian punishments on the spot immediately after an offense, *then* the state can make a significant difference in crime rates.

Vedder hastened to explain that for an economist the benefits and costs of crime can still be non-pecuniary. Rapists, for instance, gain no financial advantage from their actions. On the other hand, the costs of crime may be incurred through religious sanctions. If definitions of benefits and costs are broadened beyond a traditional accounting of dollars and cents, then an economic model can explain crime quite well, Vedder asserted.

Donohue still thought there was matter for discussion in the link between burglary and rape, earlier noted by Sampson. According to some researchers, rates for burglary, larceny, and rape run high in cities with a high turnover in population, low in cities with relatively stable populations. On the other hand, the mobility of the population in a city does not appear to make much difference for homicide, robbery, or auto theft. Donohue interpreted this as evidence that the moral integration of a city would affect planned crimes more than it would affect impulsive crimes. More broadly, Donohue conjectured that moral integration in America has eroded as the culture has lost its supports for self-denial and accepted instead an ethic of self-actualization, self-indulgence, and self-absorption.

Aware of the research Donohue cited, Hirschi nonetheless rejected the distinction between expressive and instrumental crimes as incompatible with the findings on the versatility of criminals. Besides, Sampson agreed, the difference in rates for the types of crime mentioned by Donohue can all be explained as a consequence of different opportunities for criminals, not as the result of differences in the nature of the acts committed. A high rate of population turnover would create greater social anonymity, so creating more opportunities for criminal behaviors that occur outside the home and in public spaces. Similarly, criminologists would not expect a high rate of population turnover to make much difference for offenses that typically occur inside the home. On the second issue raised by Donohue, Sampson agreed that cultural influences on self-control would make a difference on a broad scale.

Besharov intervened to try to provoke an exchange between Nicholi and Hirschi. Besharov noted that his wife, a psychotherapist, would express deep concern about so many young boys growing up without a man in their home. How will they acquire their male identity, if they ever do?

Nicholi accepted Besharov's question as basic to an understanding of crime. He noted again an abundance of psychiatric research tracing a lack of internal control to the absence of a father. Adolescents who grow up without a male role model often do cause trouble.

More skeptical, Hirschi remarked that in general criminologists do not attend to what offenders say. Most criminals are not good candidates for any kind of psychotherapy because they don't see themselves as having problems. While he could understand why an adolescent might experience exquisite anguish over not having a father, Hirschi did not expect to find such feelings often among juvenile delinquents. The problems Nicholi was addressing were probably different from those which interest criminologists. Hirschi did admit that there might be some threshold at which family life powerfully affects criminality. For instance, he noted that according to one recent study, not one of the mass murderers or serial killers of our times grew up with a father in the family. However, the number of such killers is so low that it would not affect statistical studies.

The main point, Sampson believed, was that Hirschi's theory identified lack of self-control as the primary cause of crime, while the effects of family structure on crime — in and of itself — are not as strong as some people think.

Human behavior seems very complex, Nicholi cautioned. Sociopaths with serious defects in conscience are actually quite different from delinquents who recognize that they are doing something wrong, although Nicholi did not know how often this distinction appears in research.

So far, Christensen noted, discussion of family life had focused primarily upon how parents rear their children. At a time when Americans are seeing a national retreat from marriage, evident in low marriage rates, what about the effects of family life on young adults who now marry late or not at all? Christensen cited an analysis by George Gilder, who had concluded that single men were five times more likely to commit violent crimes than married men. Does this mean that the same attitudes which prevent men from marrying also make them more violent and criminal? Or is it that many men are aggressive and prone to violence, but that after marriage their wives "domesticate" them? Does the retreat from marriage mean that Americans will start seeing more young men committing violent crimes?

Gilder's finding that single men are five times more likely to commit crime than married men — taken as a simple statistic — does not mean much, Sampson responded, since the peak ages for criminality (16 to 19) come before marriage usually occurs. In his own research, Sampson found that in and of itself marital status has no statistically measurable effect on criminality. However, among those who are married, the quality of the bond between the husband and wife is a good predictor of crime.

Reverting to an earlier point by Hirschi, Nicholi expressed puzzlement. It seemed inconceivable that criminologists would not listen to what criminals say. How can anyone really understand what is going on inside a person without listening to what he says, Nicholi asked, even if the investigator must compensate for some unreliability in what criminals say?

A survey researcher by training, Hirschi was not averse to knowing what criminals say. Yet he was nervous about asking them to account for their behavior. If they could really do that, criminologists would not be necessary. Trying to explain crime through interviews, Nock added, would provide as many explanations as there are criminals. Some researchers do interview criminals, however, Sampson reported. For instance, Jack Katz is the author of a recent book entitled *The Seductions of Crime*, based upon lengthy interviews with criminals. This approach is still fairly unrepresentative of criminology, Sampson admitted. Having piqued Chapman's curiosity, Sampson explained that Katz found that criminals generally repudiate academic theories that explain their offenses as the consequences of poverty or deprivation. Rather, criminals say they commit their offenses because of the thrills and benefits — even the fun — of the acts themselves.

Despite Sampson's earlier remarks, Carlson believed that marriage may inhibit some types of crime. Citing a recent study at Columbia and the University of California, Los Angeles, Carlson reported that when cohabiting couples married, their use of drugs fell significantly. He reasoned that once such couples started down the path of responsibility by avoiding drug use, they probably would behave more responsibly in general.

Amplifying this theme, Christensen reported that researchers at the University of New Hampshire had discovered that cohabiting women were five times as likely to suffer physical abuse as married women. This finding had surprised the researchers, who had supposed that physical abuse would occur less often among cohabiting couples because a cohabiting woman could more easily walk out. Even when cohabiting couples marry, they report lower marital satisfaction, they more often terminate their marriages in divorce, and they bear fewer children than married couples who did not cohabit. Marriage does make a difference, he concluded.

But it is the quality of marriages which affects crime, McLanahan stressed, just as it is the quality of parent-child relationships that influences delinquency. It is not very helpful simply to look at whether or not people are married or divorced or to look at whether or not children live with their fathers. It is the quality of the attachment which is decisive.

Among couples who are not married, Christensen responded, it is futile to look for quality marriages.

Nicholi rejoined the discussion to ask Hirschi whether his theoretical model applied to crimes on Wall Street and in Washington as well as to delinquency. That is *the* question constantly posed for criminologists, Hirschi admitted. The correlates of white-collar crime do parallel those for other offenses, justifying the same theoretical explanations — though Hirschi acknowledged that some of his professional colleagues remain skeptical.

Shifting from theoretical to practical concerns, Donohue asked Hirschi if he saw any implications for public policy in research finding that indicators of future criminality show up in children at fairly early ages. Hirschi replied that public officials might do more to teach parents how better to raise their children, how better to control their children's behavior.

What children need, in Peery's opinion, is a conscience. Each of us, Peery remarked, has within us the capacity to know right from wrong. That ability can be strengthened by family, by neighborhood, by other supports, but it is quality of conscience — power to know right from wrong independently — that perhaps needs more emphasis than does quality of attachments to others.

Picking up on this theme, Gecas observed that much of the discussion had focused on external control by parents, family, and others. External control may work as far as it goes, but only if children develop self-control can they be eventually released from surveillance and supervision. The questions then become: Under what conditions does conscience develop? How can parents cultivate that? Gecas identified guilt and shame as the two emotions essential to an understanding of conscience. To the extent that children do not feel guilty when they commit deviant acts, to that degree society is in trouble and must rely more heavily on external controls. However, if young people do feel guilty when they do such acts, that guilt provides a powerful motive for them to reform themselves. Development of conscience, in Gecas' view, depends upon the quality of parent-child relationships, as evident in the affection, nurturance, and support a parent gives the child and as evident in the child's identification with the parent.

External control produces internal control so that the two are not separable, Hirschi responded. The idea of conscience, he complained, carries conceptual baggage and is not theoretically fruitful. Criminologists do not usually care about guilt because it comes after the crime.

Supervision and control may give a good functional definition of prison, or at least parole, but Anderson doubted whether the family was reducible to these responsibilities. So while praising Hirschi for a powerful argument for giving parents more time for supervision and control, Anderson was not willing to dismiss conscience. Because guilt comes after a crime, it may not make any difference the first time a person commits it. But Anderson remembered times when his own guilt had inspired resolve never to repeat certain actions. Guilt does exert a deterrent effect.

Living by conscience means more than a lack of guilt and shame, Peery observed. Behavior that is compatible with conscience brings a wonderful feeling of harmony, a personal assurance that "I did that right." Parents can foster such feelings by creating a home environment of love, acceptance, and support.

Asking leave to step out of his chairman's role for a minute, Besharov complained that, for all its very great explanatory power, Hirschi's theory seems too bleak because it gives no attention to the positive attributes of human life. Humans are motivated not just by fear, not just by guilt or punishment, but also by a desire to cooperate with a larger group. People are not simply born with this desire; it grows in the family within the home.

Hirschi agreed that his explanation of criminal behavior advances theoretical understanding only up to the minimal standards of decent, civilized behavior necessary to stay out of prison. People should be intelligent, cheerful, and happy, but the cultivation of these attributes lies outside a theory of crime.

When a minor dispute began over the age at which children acquire conscience, Besharov offered the opinion that if a child has no internal control by age nine or ten, parents and others will face an uphill fight shaping such control in later years.

Nicholi agreed, yet observed that the biggest struggle in the control of impulses typically comes during adolescence. Because of the tremendous need among young adolescents to test their limits, schools see a high turnover for teachers at these ages. Teachers who are most popular with young adolescents are those who care for their students, but who are very demanding and very firm in setting limits.

Even adolescents who have internalized the right values and who will be good citizens, McLanahan commented, go through this period of struggle and rebellion.

Discipline in single-parent households is typically different from discipline in two-parent households, Nock reported, citing studies finding that single parents are more likely than married parents to exercise authoritarian discipline, forcing their children into conformity. Married parents are more often authoritative in style, encouraging their children to become compliant through self-control. The distinction between generations often disappears in single-parent families, so that the parent becomes the child's peer. Because single mothers must often rely on their children, the give and take of help and discipline is more reciprocal than in most two-parent households. Nock found it difficult to reconcile this fairly well established pattern with Hirschi's reported finding that family size determines criminality more than family structure does.

Perhaps, Hirschi responded, the differences in parenting styles found in single-parent homes vis-à-vis two-parent homes affect higher-level social relations that lie beyond the scope of criminology.

Some researchers, McLanahan reported, find that single parents use an authoritarian style in their child rearing because that style actually works better in their circumstances than the authoritative style would. In the short run, Chapman suggested, the authoritarian style is more efficient than the authoritative. Of course it is more efficient, Gecas agreed, noting studies that find that parenting styles tend to become more authoritarian as family size grows. The authoritative style of parenting is a luxury because it requires parents to sit down and reason with a child. When five other children need attention, parents often wind up simply saying, "You do it because I say so, that's why!"

Opening the final session of the conference, Christensen stressed the growth of medical costs. National health care costs — already high — could reach a trillion and a half dollars by the year 2000 and two trillion by the year 2030. Americans need to be particularly concerned about the intergenerational tensions such costs are likely to create, he warned, particularly as the baby-boom generation ages and begins to impose medical costs on the baby-bust generation. Changes in family living affect the medical costs that Americans must pay, since people who are divorced or single are less healthy than peers who are married. Not peculiar to the United States, the relationship between health and family life shows up in other countries as well. But could it be, Christensen asked, that by assuming responsibility for health care, government may be fur-

ther exacerbating weaknesses in the family — so creating more
health problems? Naturally, people do not marry in order to
improve their actuarial statistics, yet personal decisions do affect
health and medical costs. Admitting that the conclusion of his
paper is flat and unsatisfying, Christensen voiced deep reservations
not only about the welfare state, but also about insurance. He again
underscored what he perceived as a tension or polarity between
calculation and memory. While family is based upon memory,
insurance rests upon calculation. As an illustration of how these
two principles clash, Christensen drew attention to a recent ref-
erendum in San Francisco to decide whether cohabiting partners of
city employees could receive the same health-insurance coverage
given to family members. In order to bring more people under the
protection of insurance, activists were attacking received under-
standings of marriage and family.

Government has assumed a large responsibility for people's
health only recently, Christensen pointed out. In the past, government protected citizens from foreign powers and provided a sound
currency, but government did not traditionally pay medical costs
for the sick. Christensen traced the State's new willingness to care
for the sick to a utopian impulse. In his influential 19th-century
book *Looking Backward: 2000-1887*, Edward Bellamy anticipated
a time when the government would take responsibility for the first
time to see that its citizens live. Noting the age-old tension between
security and freedom, Christensen concluded by asking: How much
is our freedom compromised by making the State the guarantor of
our life and health?

Acting as discussant, Jones began his response to Christensen's
paper by reporting the comments of Ron Haskins who had original-
ly been appointed discussant for the paper, but who had been
unable to attend the conference because of his professional obligations as a staff member for the Ways and Means Committee of
the U.S. House of Representatives. Haskins stressed that correlation
is not causation: divorce and ill health may be statistically correlated, but that does not necessarily mean that *divorce* causes illness. Further, it is very difficult to do research on such questions
because an investigator cannot manipulate the marital and family
lives of a sample population in order to see what the effects might
be. Although Haskins felt that government should do more to

curtail divorce, he seriously doubted that government action would affect the divorce rate much.

Moving from Haskins' critique of the paper to his own, Jones argued that divorce does not account for most of the increase in health-care costs in recent decades. Rather, medical costs have been driven up by other influences. Medical costs have risen in large measure because those who receive health care do not usually pay the bills (at least not directly); instead, government or insurance companies pay the costs. Consequently, most people feel few restraints on their use of health care. The liability crisis has also driven up the costs of medical care. In some fields, such as gynecology and obstetrics, the cost of liability insurance has driven many doctors out of the practice. High marginal tax rates count as yet a third reason medical costs have soared, since high tax rates encourage people to shift more of their earnings into benefits such as health-care plans, which are not taxed. By shifting income into health benefits, people become overconsumers of medical care, using such care more than they would if lower tax rates gave them greater freedom in the spending of their income. Although he favored government actions to curb the divorce rate, Jones believed that containment of health costs depended mostly upon finding ways to deal with other causes of rising medical bills. Jones strongly advocated eliminating all third-party payments for medical services, so that patients themselves would have to pay market prices for the services received.

Still, Jones marvelled that in the recent debate over child care almost no attention was given to the questions Christensen raised about the public implications of family life. Jones further wondered if Congress' recent repeal of catastrophic health insurance might not open an opportunity for a broader reconsideration of social-welfare programs. For all its faults, the program for catastrophic health insurance did at least assign the costs to those people who actually benefited. Carlson interrupted to observe that the measure was repealed for precisely that reason. Jones conceded that many senior citizens did want to repeal the tax and keep the benefit, but others — including many who were covered by private programs — perceived that there was a better way to handle catastrophic medical costs. Jones concluded on a personal note, complaining that tax policies and government programs have made it difficult for him to justify, even to his son, his own sacrifice in raising seven children.

Christensen agreed with Jones that family dissolution is probably not the primary cause of rising medical costs. Those costs have risen because of an aging population and because of third-party payments for services. Litigation has also driven up medical costs: Plato recognized centuries ago that in a decadent society, hospitals and courts will multiply. However, Christensen rejected the notion that health costs were only marginally affected by family dissolution. In one recent study of chronically ill men and women over age 55, researchers discovered that married patients responded better to treatment than unmarried patients and that the hospitalization rate ran dramatically higher among the unmarried. Family dissolution places a heavier burden on public institutions for the care of the elderly. Elderly people with divorced daughters are much more likely to be in nursing homes or similar institutions than elderly people with daughters in intact marriages. Christensen also stressed that family dissolution has helped cause the birth dearth, so reducing the number of future taxpayers who will shoulder the burden of public medical expenditures.

Chapman could not shake a nagging doubt about causation. Couldn't it be that poor health causes people not to marry or not to succeed in marriage, rather than the other way around?

Although it is impossible to resolve the direction of causation clearly and decisively, Christensen observed, available evidence suggests that marriage itself fosters good health by creating a system of meaning and obligation, so that married people are less likely than unmarried people to smoke, drink, take drugs, or engage in other harmful habits. But even in studies in which the researchers only compared groups with similar health habits living in equivalent economic conditions, married people *still* enjoy a health advantage over the unmarried.

Approaching the issue from a different direction, Nock observed that the management of health care powerfully affects the structure of marriage, since health care was traditionally one of the family's central functions. Turning the task over to professionals, paid by insurance or government, the family essentially stops providing health care. The image of what a family is changes when health care no longer is a family function. Families could be empowered to provide health care, especially for the elderly, Nock remarked, if policymakers simply allowed families to be the conduits through which money flows to support elderly parents. But from a different perspective, Nock acknowledged that government has socialized health care quite effectively — that is if such things as water and sewage treatment and food inspection are recognized as health care. Most of the major declines in mortality have resulted from these types of public-health measures, often forgotten by those who focus narrowly on the doctors and medicine. If health is a public good, Nock reasoned, it is almost necessary that the state distribute or socialize some of the services which promote it. The state has socialized innoculations, for instance. In Canada and other nations with socialized medicine, the aggregate cost of medical care accounts for two or three percentage points less of the Gross National Product than in the United States.

Jones disputed the need to socialize the tasks of providing clean air, clean water, healthy milk. Free markets could provide these things without creating government monopolies, he urged — though Peery balked at the prospect of two or three competing water companies laying their pipes down the highways.

Returning to the relationship between health and divorce, Anderson recalled that during the 1970's the idea had generally prevailed that marriage, divorce, and cohabitation were private lifestyle decisions that were not properly the business of government. Government could interfere only with private decisions that caused physical or economic harm. Anderson believed the papers presented at this conference had exposed this as a false dichotomy: personal lifestyle choices entail physical and economic costs. While he did not know how far the interrelationship could be pursued, Anderson thought it appropriate to reconsider community supports for marriage and sanctions against divorce.

Jones' critique of Christensen's paper, Carlson complained, had obscured the broader picture. The central issue is the futility of tinkering with the welfare state as a way of helping the family. The fundamental problem is that the welfare state exists as a substitute for the family and it only exists as that. Family decay feeds the growth of the welfare state. Carlson seconded Christensen's criticism of insurance companies. The insurance company is a modern invention designed to replace the uncertainties of families with the rigid certainty of an institution. Deconstructing the welfare state would make rearing children economically and socially rational

again by allowing the natural family to reemerge. If Social Security, Medicare, and Medicaid were all abolished, along with the labor
laws that restrict what children can do, the family would do quite
well in the primary economy that would develop, since a family
provides security, a family provides more hands, and a family can
provide a division of labor among its members. Admitting that he
had just outlined an implausible political scenario, Carlson proposed as an alternative strategy the overthrow of the Tax Reform
Act of 1986, bringing back higher income-tax rates with income-
splitting for married couples and substantial deductions. Such a
policy would effectively transfer the nation's tax burden to people
without children, so that families would be relatively better off —
even if the nation as a whole declines.

Lest he be misunderstood, Jones said that he fully accepted the
bill of indictment against the welfare state in Christensen's paper
and had himself been trying for years to dismantle the welfare
bureaucracy.

Endorsing Jones' analysis of the health-care crisis, Vedder
identified third-party payments and the tax system as far more
important than family dissolution in causing health costs to rise.
Yet he accepted Christensen's argument that divorce causes poor
health rather than the other way around. By any measure health
has improved during the 20th century, but rates for divorce have
soared. If poor health caused divorce, improved health should have
helped hold divorce down.

In response to Carlson's remarks, Vedder stressed the differences between small incremental change and drastic change. In the
tax debate of the 1980's, policymakers finally abandoned incremental
tinkering in favor of a radical change no one could have anticipated
ten years ago. The Tax Reform Act of 1986 was a rare instance when
the general interest overwhelmed the special interests. Can the
general interest — which Vedder characterized as pro-family and
anti-divorce — overwhelm special interests to effect a significant
restructuring of the welfare state? Vedder did not expect it to
happen, but he refused to rule it out of the question.

Unconvinced by Vedder's reasoning on the relationship between
health and divorce, Chapman contended that it is relative, not
absolute health which determines the prospects of marriage or the
likelihood of divorce. A person who is *relatively* unhealthy will find

it hard to marry, even if everyone else is unhealthier than we see in the contemporary world.

In any case, Besharov interjected, official divorce rates before 1965 or 1970 do not tell the whole story, since many people who were separated from spouses were still counted as married. Even by official statistics and even under the rigid divorce laws prevailing before the adoption of "no fault" statutes, divorce rates reached a peak right after World War II that was almost as high as we see right now.

For Besharov, Christensen's paper raised fundamental questions about people who — whether because of personality or lifestyle choice — are less expensive to society than other people. Many of the same arguments used about marriage and parenthood could apply to smokers and nonsmokers. Because smokers cost society more, many people feel that smokers should pay higher taxes and insurance premiums and should be given fewer chances to receive heart transplants and other similar operations. Americans do often distinguish between the deserving and the undeserving sick. Christensen's paper raises the possibility that policymakers could justify a special tax status for the family on the basis of objective evidence, not simply as a way of saying they believe in families or as a punitive measure against folks who are not married.

But what about the lawsuits filed against insurance companies that charge married people lower premiums than they charge unmarried people? Jones asked. Congress is even considering legislation that would make it more difficult for insurance companies to provide lower premiums for nonsmokers than for smokers.

Anderson was reminded of a Supreme Court case in the early 1970's, *New Jersey Welfare Rights Organization* v. *Cahill*, in which the High Court ruled that the state could not deny any welfare benefits on the basis of marriage or living arrangements. In handing down its opinion, the Supreme Court said that any distinction between a family based on marriage and other living arrangement was irrational. Anderson felt that this conference had supplied a rational reason, with empirical evidence, to support the family based upon marriage.

Despite this logic, Jones saw political currents still moving against the family — as in San Francisco's recent attempt to provide health insurance benefits to cohabiting partners of city employees. Far from favoring this initiative, insurance companies were horrified by the possibility of its enactment, since it would have distorted the real purpose of insurance by making actuarial tables impossible to calculate.

Questions of health, McLanahan insisted, must be assessed separately from questions of health costs. It does not appear that divorce could be significantly injuring health during a century when longevity has risen markedly at the same time divorce rates have also risen. On the other hand, divorce has reduced the ability of families to care for elderly parents, so shifting the costs of their care to the state.

Christensen countered that because of new medical technology, longevity would have risen even higher had it not been for divorce. Unpersuaded, McLanahan noted a study, cited in Christensen's own paper, showing that after age 60 marriage is not as important in keeping people healthy as is simply having social support. In McLanahan's view this was evidence that the correlation between morbidity and marital status below age 60 reflects the failure of people with bad health habits to marry; it does not show that divorce causes serious illness. Further, since people 60 and over are the group chiefly responsible for driving medical costs up, McLanahan judged it a mistake to blame this rise in costs on illness caused by singleness or divorce.

Regardless of the rational reasons for strengthening the family, Donohue predicted a continuing fight on family issues between general vs. special interest, elite vs. public opinion. Whereas the general public still supports traditional moral values, elite opinion does not. Rather, in the nation's media, academy, and non-profit sector, the New Class of opinion-makers espouses tolerance toward extramarital sex and other deviations from traditional norms. This clash between popular opinion and elite opinion has meant ongoing cultural warfare in America, a civil war of sorts, in Donohue's assessment.

Carlson drew a distinction between social insurance and actuarial insurance, seeing in the difference between these two types of insurance an illustration of Christensen's point that policymakers must either impose values or impose collectivized costs. Actuarial insurance allows those who live by certain values to purchase their insurance at a cheaper rate than those who violate those values, who may still buy insurance but at a higher price. The great dilemma of the welfare state is that social insurance works well so long as society possesses a large fund of moral capital provided by strong families and responsible individuals. For a time, a welfare state will operate well by drawing on society's moral capital. However, over time the very mechanism of the welfare state absorbs and burns up society's moral capital. Because of this exhaustion of moral resources, some of the Scandinavian states now face a crisis of sorts in trying to find ways to continue to pay for their welfare systems. Some Scandinavian leaders are trying to persuade people to take care of the chronically ill — old and young — and the severely handicapped in their homes, because care in the home is cheaper. However, Scandinavian citizens are finding it very difficult to think that way again now that they have learned that the state will assume the burden of caring for family members. Once virtue and vice receive equal treatment under social insurance, it is very difficult to reconstruct a society in which people accept the kind of individual sacrifice required to care for a sick or retarded person in the home. Actuarial insurance could offer a way out of the dilemma by basing the cost of protection on the virtues of the individual, although Carlson doubted whether the Supreme Court would allow such distinctions under current interpretations of the 14th Amendment.

Appealing for concrete proposals to strengthen families, McLanahan saw little point in further discussions about abolishing the welfare state, something she did not believe was going to happen. In any case, social insurance affects the elderly far more than it does young families, and it is among young families that most divorces occur. Young couples do not even think of Social Security or health insurance in making family decisions. There are many other social and economic forces pulling couples apart and parents away from children.

The contemporary family is often an empty shell, Anderson explained, because the family has been drained of its social and economic foundations over the last several decades. He could not believe that families are strengthened by government services which substitute for family functions. Rather, Americans need to look for mechanisms that would enable the family to perform its own functions. For instance, the tax code could be changed to give families more disposable income. Also worth investigating are policy changes so that more health care can be provided in the home. Where officials have taken children on respirators out of the hospitals and allowed them to be cared for at home, the arrangement has been more economical than hospital care and has helped the family. More such policies could be adopted.

Besharov saw some difficulty in pursuing the kind of strategy Anderson advocated because of the current politics of family issues. He noted that the debate over day care in the United States has been shaped by home arrangements which he described as "a third, a third, a third" — roughly a third of American mothers have chosen to work full time, about a third of American mothers have chosen not to work outside the home, and approximately one third have chosen to work part time. But Besharov reported that recently the third group has been disappearing, as many mothers who worked part time, waiting until their children turn 3 or 4 or 5, have started working full time. In the situation that is emerging, the question of maternal employment will split American families into two almost evenly divided groups. Besharov regarded the situation as one of worrisome polarization, a civil war of sorts that policymakers ought to try to defuse. For that reason, tax credits made the most sense to Besharov because such credits allow support for both types of families. Besharov saw the cleavage in American society over maternal employment in the passage of two different versions of a day-care bill by the House of Representatives. Even behind closed doors, the House cannot choose between stay-at-home mothers and mothers employed full time — so it passes two different day-care bills.

Family-rights groups, in Vedder's view, are missing an opportunity by not exploiting the rhetoric of motherhood and family enough. Despite the growth in the proportion of people living outside of traditional family arrangements, there is still residual support for the family in America. Why hasn't anyone seriously proposed a "Family Rights Amendment" to the Constitution giving legal protection to the nuclear family? Perhaps a Constitutional Amendment is not the right strategy for advocates of the family, but rhetoric is very important to the charisma, the strong feelings about families necessary for sweeping changes. What politician would vote against family rights? Vedder asked.

The White House Conference on Families offered discouraging proof for Donohue that a rhetoric of "family" could go awry.

Convened by President Jimmy Carter as a way to strengthen the
family, the conference could not even agree on what the term *family*
means.

Peery expressed faith that individuals would react rationally on
family issues if given correct information. He deplored the absence
from current textbooks of the kind of information presented at this
conference on developmental psychology and marriage and the
family. Those who know this information bear a moral obligation to
set the record straight. Not willing to give up on the possibility of
radical reform, Peery thought that the repeal of catastrophic health
care illustrated what could happen with social-welfare legislation
if Congress always clearly identified who was receiving benefits
and who was paying for them. The specter of huge federal deficits
may also help Congress and the American people to realize that the
system is a little out of control: cuts in spending are necessary and
right.

Democracy, Christensen acknowledged, requires trust that, on
balance, people will behave rationally when they know the facts.
However, there is a difference between rationality and rationalism.
Emile Durkheim observed that individualism and rationalism
parallel one another in development and one will reinforce the
other. The risks of rationalist individualism ought to be borne in
mind by those considering health care and the family. Conceding
that the state is fairly effective in the health services it provides just
as insurance companies are quite effective in protecting clients
against risk, Christensen again noted that moral excellence and
economic efficiency are in tension with one another. Extended
kinship in pre-industrial societies was not very efficient in providing care and protection, while the state may be very effective in
prolonging the lives of deracinated individuals. But modern efficiency appeared problematic to Christensen, who also worried
about the preservation of freedom in a welfare state. Since the cost
of freedom has always been suffering and death, the pursuit of
health as the highest good could mean that Americans will surren-
der everything to the state in order to guarantee health. Freedom
requires hard choices, including a willingness to die. Christensen
recalled the public outcry when Governor Richard Lamm reminded
Americans that people do have to die. (Lamm, Jones protested, had
not simply said people have to die. Lamm said older people have a
duty to die, to get out of the way.) After a recent personal experience

with a man who died of congestive heart failure after heroic, protracted, costly, and finally unsuccessful medical efforts, Christensen wondered if resistance to mortality had not become almost obscene.

Returning the discussion to the social costs of divorce, Anderson proposed that policies be changed to shift more of the costs of divorce from women to men. Under current arrangements, affluent men actually benefit from divorce. The 50-50 division of marital property often means that the wife receives half of the assets to share with three or four children, while the husband alone receives the other half. The economic status of women and children declines markedly after divorce, while the economic status of men either dips slightly or rises significantly. While a 45- or 50-year-old divorced man can find another wife easily, a 45- or 50-year-old woman faces a much harder time finding a new spouse. Anderson criticized "no fault" divorce for serving only the interests of the spouse who wants the marriage dissolved, not the interests of the spouse who wants the marriage to survive nor the interests of the children. This imbalance deserves scrutiny, Anderson concluded.

Besharov questioned this assessment of contemporary divorce law in that Anderson assumed that children are a cost. From an economist's perspective, the divorce may be viewed as the mother's purchase of the children from the father. Although he agreed with Anderson about how divorce law ought to be reformed, Besharov reported that divorce litigation often amounts to the sale of the children — however much we may dislike such sales for social reasons.

McLanahan objected that it is not fair to the children to allow a divorcing mother to "buy" her children in divorce negotiations, since it economically harms the children. Someone must protect the interests of the children of divorcing parents.

Contemporary custody policies — which almost automatically assign custody to divorcing mothers — are an incentive to divorce, Chapman remarked. In the 19th century, the courts usually assigned custody to the party least likely to want the children, namely the father. This practice provided an incentive for both parties to stay in the marriage: a father could not make a clean getaway; a mother could not leave without surrendering what she values most, her children. Perhaps, Chapman concluded, the courts should not automatically grant custody to mothers.

When assessing the costs of divorce, Nock suggested, it makes sense to consider a man's future earnings, since the average length for a marriage that ends in divorce is only seven years — too short for most couples to have accumulated much property. It should also be remembered that state laws allow for two different types of divorce settlements. In eight states, "community property" statutes govern divorce negotiations, usually leaving the woman much worse off after divorce than before. Most states govern divorce settlements under an "equitable division" system (traceable, Nock supposed, to Napoleonic tradition) that protects women's economic interests better than "community property" statutes. Equitable division of contested property is done by the court in recognition of each spouse's particular needs and past contributions.

In the waning moments of the conference, Peery reflected on its significance, quoting two verses from the Old Testament in summation: "It is not good that the man should be alone" (Gen. 2:18) and "the iniquity of the fathers [shall be visited] upon the children" (Ex. 20:5).

Accepting this scriptural conclusion to the proceedings, Besharov adjourned the conference.

Index